This is the fascinating true story of two brothers, Johan and Karl Hermann, who came from Germany in the 1850's to settle on the American frontier in Arkansas.

Seeking to make a new life for themselves, they befriended the native Cherokee Indians, established a thriving grain mill, named their settlement Hermannsburg (now Dutch Mills), married two sisters from Germany and raised their children.

In their letters and diaries, they describe in vivid detail how they embraced, endured, and exulted in the rigors of their newfound lives until the deadly American Civil War battles which raged around them forced them to relinquish their beloved town and relocate to the city of St. Louis, where many of their descendants became prominent families of that burgeoning city and flourish there today.

I beckon you now to retrace their journey, to relive their amazing experiences of joy, sorrow, romance and triumph on the American frontier, carving out new lives in an exciting new world.

Frederick A. Hermann III
St. Louis, MO
June, 2012

THE HERMANNS

OF OLD HERMANNSBURG

Washington County,

Arkansas

Compiled and edited

by W J. LEMKE

Published by the

WASHINGTON COUNTY HISTORICAL SOCIETY

Fayetteville, Arkansas

1965

OUR THANKS

to W. E. Meyer of State College, Pennsylvania, and to
Wolfgang Gscheidlen of Stuttgart, Germany, who sent us
much previously unpublished material pertaining to the
Hermanns and who loaned us most of the pictures that
appear in this booklet.

And if our booklet needs a dedication, it is to

NANNI HERMANN

whose picture (silhouette) appears on the cover. She
wrote a diary in Washington County, Arkansas, in 1862;
Fled with her children from Civil War violence; and
died in Washington, Missouri, April 30, 1863.

Her story furnished the initial inspiration for my
Hermann research.

— W. J. Lemke

THE HERMANNS' FIRST LOG HOME
at Old Hermannsburg, Washington County, Arkansas

(This photo came to us from Wolfgang Gscheidlen of Stuttgart, Germany, who got it from his sister Hedi, who got it from Anita Hermann Bilharz of Baxter Springs, Kansas, who got it from Ruth Leach, postmaster at Dutch Mills, Arkansas.)

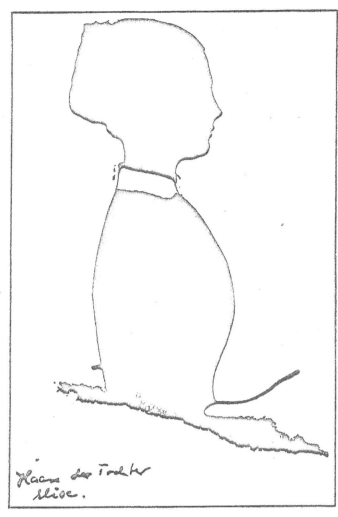

Haare der Tochter Alice.

NANNI HERMANN

In the University Library there is a privately printed book that gives the history of a group of German families who came to Northwest Arkansas in 1850 and founded the village of Hermannsburg (now Dutch Mills) in western Washington County. Prominent among them were two brothers named Jean and Karl Hermann.

They carried on agriculture, a store, a mill, and other industries. They lived on good terms with the neighbors and were held in high esteem as peaceful and honest folks. They were well on their way to becoming prosperous, when the first signs of approaching civil war appeared. They tried to remain neutral, but they were gradually taken to be abolitionists and were considered enemies of the South.

From 1860 to 1862 they were in constant danger from the opposing armies and especially from the thieving and murdering bushwhackers who overran northwest Arkansas. In the fall of 1862 it became evident that continued existence at Hermannsburg was impossible, so the Herman brothers and their families made ready to flee for safety to St. Louis.

They secured a cavalry escort from General Blunt, the Union commander. They left Cane Hill December 18 in four army wagons, taking only absolute necessities and leaving everything else behind.

The group numbered 19, including eleven children from 1 year to 9 years old. The Hermanns reached General Herron's camp at Prairie Grove on December 19. He gave them an order permitting them to travel with a commissary train to Fayetteville and on to Rolla. The following paragraph is a translation from the German dairy of Nanni, wife of one of the Hermann brothers:

"We left Prairie Grove on December 24 and reached Fayetteville that same day. We camped near a spring at the north end of that village, where we spent Christmas day. But the Christ-child had lost its magic. Looking up at the star-studded sky on Christmas Eve, our memory saw again the lighted Christmas trees in our distant Fatherland."

Nanni did not live to reach St. Louis. She died on the journey, leaving her husband with two small children, age 2 and 5, both born in Washington County.

The spot where these 19 refugees spent their heartsick Christmas in 1862 was Big Spring on E. Spring street, which is just across the creek from the Lemke home. On Christmas Eve I shall walk out in my back yard and look across the ravine. And I shall remember two mothers— Nanni Hermann with her babies, sleeping in a wagon bed in Fayetteville, and Mary with her Baby, asleep in a stable in Bethlehem.   —WJL

INTRODUCTORY NOTES on the HERMANN STORY

by W. J. Lemke

I first saw Dutch Mills in the spring of 1929. I was on my way to locate the site of Old Vineyard, about a mile north of Evansville and our county's first postoffice (1829). I turned off the highway at the crossing of the Barren Fork and spent the rest of the day learning my Dutch Mills a-b-c's. I learned that the name of the village came from an ante-bellum settlement of German immigrants (1850). The original name of the U.S. postoffice was Hermannsburg.

One thing led to another, and presently I was involved in one of our county's most romantic stories — the story of Old Hermannsburg. The story has everything — pioneer hardships and industry, war-time violence, buried treasure. And all of it documented, because the Hermanns wrote letters and kept diaries that are still in existence today, more than a century after.

It didn't take me long to learn the legends of Dutch Mills, from such old-timers as Mrs. Ruth Leach, Dutch Mills postmaster who lives on the site of the first log house built by John Hermann. This was also the Reed home 70 years ago, where my good friend, Jack Reed, spent his childhood. I'm sure that Mrs. Leach and Mr. Reed will recognize the picture, showing the country road winding up the hill behind today's main street. Our Washington County Historical Society has placed a historical marker on the old road.

But I've heard interesting tales before. So, I wanted Dutch Mills documented. I found several books in the University library, printed in German, which I read and translated. I do not remember how I got in touch with Prof. W.E.Meyer of Pennsylvania State University, who is a Hermann kinsman. He put me in touch with another descendant, Wolfgang Gscheidlen of Stuttgart, Germany, who owns many of the original Hermannsburg records. I have had much correspondence with Professor Meyer and Herr Gscheidlen. I shall quote from their letters, where the information is not available elsewhere.

For example: When John Hermann came to Washington County in 1850, he worked a year for Hermann Freyschlag at the latter's mill. His letters suggest that the Freyschlag mill was located on Clear Creek and later became the Pegram mill. The Freyschlags made the Gold Rush to California and John Hermann moved to what is now Dutch Mills. Freyschlag information is hard to come by, but our WCHS Flashback has published (Jan. 1954) the account of the Freyschlags' ownership of what is now the main campus of the University of Arkansas.

John Hermann's acquisition of the mill site at Old Hermannsburg (now Dutch Mills) is well documented. The unfinished mill was on the hittaker Branch that flowed fromthe hittaker Spring into the Barren Fork river. The spring is still there (1965) but there is not enough water to turn a mill wheel. But what discourages me is that I have been unable to learn anything about the hittakers. I think they were late-comers — after the War — because the Hermanns never mentioned the name hittaker.

5

There are other questions pertaining to Old Hermannsburg. The record testifies that at least one (possibly two) of the family's "buried treasures" was never found. Yet tradition has it that one post-War citizen bought a farm and paid for it with $5,000 in gold. This is strictly legend, but it is believed by some Dutch Mills old-timers. I think I can get one affidavit, but that's not enough for historical proof.

I am also interested in the old cemetery behind the Liberty Baptist Church at Dutch Mills. The first burials, on what was undoubtedly the Hermanns' land were those of the Rev. Wilhelmi Wilhelmi, father-in-law of the founders of Hermannsburg -- Johann and Karl Hermann, and of his daughter-in-law who was the wife of his son Julius Wilhelmi.

The Dutch Mills cemetery, whose western boundary line is the state line between Arkansas and Oklahoma, was donated for cemetery purposes by the Weber family. There is a historical marker at the entrance that tells of the Webers. The Wilhelmis have no marker in the Dutch Mills cemetery, an oversight that we hope to correct soon.

While speculating on the neglect of the pioneers, I thought of the miller Dannenberg, who operated two mills in Washington County but was tied to a tree in Evansville and whittled to death by Indian tomahawks. I can furnish one afficavit -- "My grandmother told me." That's not good enough, until I learn where the Dannenberg descendants are.

There are other Washington County pioneers mentioned in the Hermann records, such as Stephen K. Stone, the Freyschlags, Thomas H. Tennnant, and others. All of these deserve more historical research and attention than they have received in the past.

This, then, is an account of a German settlement in Washington County, Arkansas, that showed great promise but lasted only a dozen years. Hermannsburg was a casualty of the Civil War.

THE HERMANNS OF OLD HERMANNSBURG

JOHN H. HERMANN
as a European engineer

JOHN H. HERMANN
as a St. Louis doctor

KARL FRIEDRICH HERMANN who married LINA WILHELMI
John H. Hermann was the founder of Old Hermannsburg (now Dutch Mills). He built
the mill and established the settlement. He was joined later by his brother Karl. The
Hermann brothers, John H. and Karl F. married sisters, Nanni and Lina Wilhelmi of Gray's
Summit, Mo. All lived in Washington County, Ark., and their children were born here.

JOHANN HEINRICH HERMANN as a young man in Germany

NANNI WILHELMI who married **JOHANN HEINRICH HERMANN**

J. H. Hermann was the founder of Old Hermannsburg, now Dutch Mills, in Washington County, Arkansas. The silhouettes were supplied by their descendants, Wolfgang Gscheidlen in Stuttgart, Germany, and Prof. W. E. Meyer of Pennsylvania State College.

Descendant Chart for
Johann Heinrich HERMANN

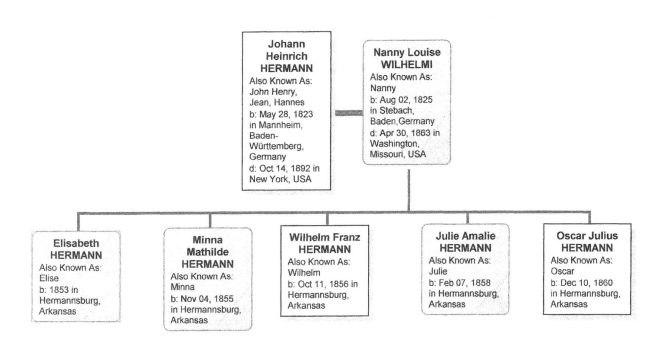

Johann Heinrich HERMANN
Also Known As:
John Henry,
Jean, Hannes
b: May 28, 1823
in Mannheim,
Baden-
Württemberg,
Germany
d: Oct 14, 1892 in
New York, USA

Nanny Louise WILHELMI
Also Known As:
Nanny
b: Aug 02, 1825
in Stebach,
Baden, Germany
d: Apr 30, 1863 in
Washington,
Missouri, USA

Elisabeth HERMANN
Also Known As:
Elise
b: 1853 in
Hermannsburg,
Arkansas

Minna Mathilde HERMANN
Also Known As:
Minna
b: Nov 04, 1855
in Hermannsburg,
Arkansas

Wilhelm Franz HERMANN
Also Known As:
Wilhelm
b: Oct 11, 1856 in
Hermannsburg,
Arkansas

Julie Amalie HERMANN
Also Known As:
Julie
b: Feb 07, 1858
in Hermannsburg,
Arkansas

Oscar Julius HERMANN
Also Known As:
Oscar
b: Dec 10, 1860
in Hermannsburg,
Arkansas

Descendant Chart for
Karl Friedrich HERMANN

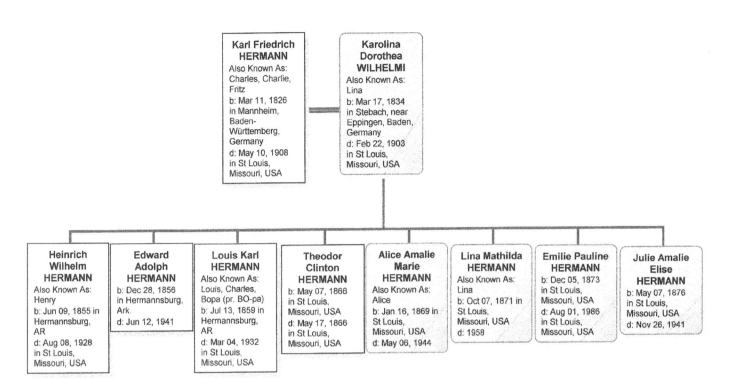

Karl Friedrich HERMANN
Also Known As: Charles, Charlie, Fritz
b: Mar 11, 1826 in Mannheim, Baden-Württemberg, Germany
d: May 10, 1908 in St Louis, Missouri, USA

Karolina Dorothea WILHELMI
Also Known As: Lina
b: Mar 17, 1834 in Stebach, near Eppingen, Baden, Germany
d: Feb 22, 1903 in St Louis, Missouri, USA

Heinrich Wilhelm HERMANN
Also Known As: Henry
b: Jun 09, 1855 in Hermannsburg, AR
d: Aug 08, 1928 in St Louis, Missouri, USA

Edward Adolph HERMANN
b: Dec 28, 1856 in Hermannsburg, Ark.
d: Jun 12, 1941

Louis Karl HERMANN
Also Known As: Louis, Charles, Bopa (pr. BO-pa)
b: Jul 13, 1859 in Hermannsburg, AR
d: Mar 04, 1932 in St Louis, Missouri, USA

Theodor Clinton HERMANN
b: May 07, 1866 in St Louis, Missouri, USA
d: May 17, 1866 in St Louis, Missouri, USA

Alice Amalie Marie HERMANN
Also Known As: Alice
b: Jan 16, 1869 in St Louis, Missouri, USA
d: May 06, 1944

Lina Mathilda HERMANN
Also Known As: Lina
b: Oct 07, 1871 in St Louis, Missouri, USA
d: 1958

Emilie Pauline HERMANN
b: Dec 05, 1873 in St Louis, Missouri, USA
d: Aug 01, 1986 in St Louis, Missouri, USA

Julie Amalie Elise HERMANN
b: May 07, 1876 in St Louis, Missouri, USA
d: Nov 26, 1941

EARLY SETTLERS OF DUTCH MILLS

(List compiled by W. /Scheidlen)   L Gscheidlen

I have tried to list the Germans who lived in Hermannsburg, in the 1850s. The list is probably incomplete and you may want to make corrections.

Johann Hermann and family
Karl F. Hermann and family
The Fischers - George and his brother Adam and his sister Elise
The Rev. Eberle and his family
The Wilhelmi families
George Hackinjos
The Dannenbergs
Rassmus (of Washington, Mo.) who worked with Karl Hermann and
        married daughter of Dannenberg
The Webers (Johann, M., Liese. Liese Weber was maid-servant in
        the Johann Hermann household
Crozius, justice of the peace; murdered during the Civil War.
Kragt, chief miller
Rhein, stoker in the mill
Dietrich, who lived in Julius Wilhelmi's house
Joseph Schmitt, employed by Karl Hermann
    S. Albert   still 1862
    {lives with family}

Also living in the general area were the following native American families:
Frank Weatherspoon, whose house stood on the Barren Fork, between
        the two fords
Jake White
James Gage
M. Inks
El Leach
Bob Whinnery
Gert Burrow, who had two boys
Rev. Thomas H. Tennant, neighbor of Karl Hermann
J. M. Chandler
M. P. English, who died 1867
Evans, who lived 2½ miles north of the mill
George Washington, employed by Karl Hermann
Ira Williams, who built new house in 1866, 1 mile north of mill
Legg, who was a neighbor of Karl Hermann
Earle, a Captain in the Confederate army
Russell, who ran away with $10,000 borrowed money but later returned
Sparks, a thief who left Hermannsburg during the War
The Reed and Cox families
The McCarthy family
James Hukill, first postmaster
Of the foregoing, the following were murdered during the Civil War: Weatherspoon, White, Gage, Inks, Leach, Whinnery, and others.

(Editor's note: Names of the native Americans who
lived in the Hermannsburg area have been documented. However, some lived a considerable distance
from Hermannsburg. Thus, Capt.Earle's home was at
Cane Hill (8 miles); Chandler lived 5 miles south;
and the Reeds and Coxes lived south of Cane Hill.)

NOTES ON HERMANN NAMES

The founder of Old Hermannsburg was Johann Heinrich Hermann, known to
the native Americans as John Henry. He was also called Jean by some of
his relatives and he always signed his letters, to his mother in Germany
as "Hannes." This is a diminutive of his first name Johann and was used
by the Germans in an affectionate way.

His brother at Hermannsburg was Karl Friedrich Hermann, who went by his
second name and was called "Fritz" by his kinsmen. He had the first store
at Old Hermannsburg and was called "Charlie" by many of the natives, a
term which he resented.

The name of Johann Heinrich Hermann's wife is spelled variously, as
Nanny, Nani and Nannie. Her sister, the wife of Karl Friedrich Hermann,
was Lina. They had a sister named Minna. There is no variation in spell-
ing of these names and Nanni signed her name usually as "Nanni."

"Aunt Luise", in the Wilhelmi records, was the wife of Julius Wilhelmi,
and thus sister-in-law of Nanni and Lina Hermann. Luise's death was the
first in the family. The father of the sisters, Rev. Wilhelm Wilhelmi,
died in 1860, and is buried in the Dutch Mills cemetery.

"LONGER THAN A LIFETIME IN MISSOURI"
Excerpts from Goebel: "Longer than a Lifetime in Missouri", pp.12,16,152.

In the year 1850 a group of Germans, all industrious and well educated, migranted to northwest Arkansas, close to the line of the Indian
Territory. They bought property there and called their village Hermannsburg. There was no unified organization. Each was independent of
the others and made his own living, but many of the families were related.
They carried on agriculture, a mill, and a wool-carding machine, a
store and other industries. They lived on good terms with their neighbors and also with the partially civilized Cherokees. They were held
in high esteem as peaceful and honest folks.

They were well on their way to become prosperous or even wealthy,
when the first signs of approaching civil war appeared. They tried to
remain neutral and even discontinued their German newspapers, since
many people thought all Germans were abolitionists.

In the fall elections of 1860 they did not vote for Lincoln but for
Breckenridge. However, they were gradually taken to be abolitionists
and were considered enemies of the South. Their situation in this
isolated region was extremely dangerous. Thieving and murdering bushwhackers overran northwest Arkansas. Because of the impossibility of
making their way to a refuge at St. Louis, these German families spent
nearly two years in fear and danger. Their men folks were in constant
danger, and had to spend their nights hidden in the forest.

After the advance of the Union army under Generals Blunt and Herron,
in the fall of 1862, it became evident that continued existence at
Hermannsburg was impossible and the Hermanns and other families made
ready to flee for safety to their fellow countrymen near St.Louis.

THE ROMANTIC STORY
OF OLD HERMANNSBURG (now Dutch Mills)

by W. J. Lemke

(Reprinted from Flashback, Volume IX, No.3)

One of Washington County's romantic bits of history is the story of
Hermannsburg, now called Dutch Mills. This community was settled in
the early 1850s by a number of immigrant families from Germany, among
them the Hermanns, Wilhelmi, Dieterich, Ganter, Schmidt, Dannenberg, *⌐Dietrich*
Weber, Eberle, Kraft and others whose names have been forgotten.

Many of these were educated persons and skilled craftsmen. The lead-
ers of the settlement were the Hermann brothers, John and Karl. The
brothers married sisters — daughters of the Rev. Wilhelm Wilhelmi who
had brought his family to Franklin County, Missouri in 1850. The Wilhelmi family later joined their daughters and sons-in-law in Washing-
to County, Arkansas.

The prosperity and happiness of the German settlers on the Indian
border came to an end in 1861. Situated as they were, on the route of
both Southern and Northern armies, and vulnerable to both bushwhackers
and Indian renegades, They were in constant danger. So they left, *⌐they*
seeking refuge in St.Louis. The last group (19 persons) left Hermannsburg in December 1862, shortly after the battle of Prairie Grove.

After the war the name of Hermannsburg was changed to Dutch Mills.
The "Dutch" is a misnomer. These settlers were from south Germany, far
removed from any Dutch connections. The word "Dutch" was employed as a
derogatory term by Southern sympathizers in northwest Arkansas, after
the appearance of St. Louis German regiments in General Franz Sigel's
army at Pea Ridge in March 1862.

A surprising thing about the history of Hermannsburg is that surviv-
ors of the settlement wrote and published, both in St.Louis and in
Germany, accounts of their 12 years in Washington County, Arkansas. It
is from these writings that our account is taken. The pamphlets and
books, as well as the original source materials (letters and diaries),
are in German.

I first saw the Barren Fork river and the site of Old Hermannsburg
35 years ago. Since then, I have read everything I could find on this
German settlement that ended in war-time disaster. Luckily I was able
to contact descendants of the Hermanns who sent me information about
the family that had been published in Germany and that I could not
have obtained without their help.

The most dramatic material pertaining to Old Hermannsburg is in the
diaries kept by the Wilhelmi sisters, Nanni and Lina — the wives of
John and Karl Hermann — during the war years of 1861-62. We are publishing these, because they give a stark picture of civil war and the
⌐noncombatants unenviable position of noncombatants. Names of historic personages
are plentiful — McCulloch and Marmaduke of the Confederate army,
Blunt and Herron of the Federal army, Freyschlag and Stephen K. Stone,
Washington County pioneers.

The story includes such highlights as a 43-day crossing of the Atlantic; an 8-day trip from Pittsburgh, Pa. to Napoleon, Ark., and two more weeks to VanBuren; a buying trip to New Orleans when the steamer Forrest City exploded her boilers; on the Mississippi; the murder of the Fischer brothers; bushwhacker raids; buried treasure, Christmas Eve in Fayetteville 1862.

For background, there is published below an excerpt from Gert Goebel's book, "Longer Than a Lifetime in Missouri". Also, biographies of the two principal actors in the Hermannsburg story, John and Karl Hermann. This introduction will be followed by the diaries of Nanni and Lina Hermann, written in Washington County in 1862 and on the flight north that ended with Nanni's death at Washington, Mo. The diaries will be followed by Karl Hermann's account of the search in 1863 for the gold they had buried at their old home in Washington County.

--- H ---

(Editor's note: Since the publication of the foregoing in the Washington County Historical Society's "Flashback", we have obtained copies of other valuable material, including the childhood memories of Elise Hermann Nuessle of Germany, and the Hermann family letters written in 1862. These came to us through courtesy of W.E.Meyer, professor in State College, Pennsylvania, a descendant of the Hermanns, and from Herr Gscheidlen of Stuttgart, Germany. All are in German, and I had some trouble in translating them, not with vocabulary but with the formal and stylized sentence structure of a hundred years ago. After all, I've been an Arkansawyer for 36 years and have had little opportunity to practice my German. Or my French and Spanish, for that matter. -- WJL)

--- H ---

JOHANN HEINRICH HERMANN

Johann Heinrich Hermann was born May 28, 1823 in Mannheim, Germany. He studied engineering in the Vienna Polytechnic and at the University of Heidelberg and worked in large manufacturing plants in Germany, Belgium and France.

Driven out of France by the revolution of 1848, he went to Switzerland where he met a Heidelberg schoolmate named Gantner. The latter emigrated to America and was soon followed by Hermann.

They arrived in Washington County, Arkansas, in 1850 and bought several hundred acres of land and a site for a mill. They did almost everything, including the practice of medicine. Hermann gained a wide reputation for his cures, although he used only WATER.

Johann Hermann married the daughter of Rev. Wilhelm Wilhelmi from Baden, Germany, who with his wife and two daughters had migrated to America in 1850, to live with his two sons who had fled as a result of the Baden revolution of 1849 and had settled on a farm near Gray's Summit, Missouri.

Johann Hermann started a German settlement in western Washington County, Arkansas, near the Indian line, secured a postoffice by the name of Hermannsburg, and sold building lots.

In 1855 his brother-in-law, Julius Wilhelmi, associated himself with him and they converted the water mill which Hermann had built into a steam mill. They also installed wool-carding machines. Both enterprises were successful until the start of the Civil War.

Hermann's wife died as a result of the hardships of 1860 to 1862 and he returned to Germany in 1863. He then completed his studies in medicine at Heidelberg and returned to America in 1865, becoming a physician in St.Louis. Because of eye trouble, he retired from his medical practice in 1884, went to Germany, but returned to America in 1889. He died October 14, 1892 in New York City.

His children were Wilhelm Franz, born October 11, 1856 in Hermannsburg, Washington County, Arkansas. W.F. married Johanna Bang and they had three daughters. He was a dentist in St.Louis. The second son was Oskar Julius, ~~born~~ *born* Dec. 10, 1860 in Hermannsburg. Oskar had three sons and two daughters. Until 1892 he was an electrician in Emden, New Jersey, then moved to a fruit farm in Georgia.

KARL ~~HEINRICH~~ *Friedrich* HERMANN

Karl ~~Heinrich~~ *Friedrich* Hermann was born March 11, 1826 in Mannheim, Germany. He became a designer in a silk factory in Lyons, France, but homesickness took him back to Germany. He then served four years as a bookkeeper in Stuttgart. He was working in a bank ~~in Germany~~ *L of Lyons, France* when the outbreak of the French revolution in 1846 caused the dismissal of three-fourths of the employees. Many of them, including Hermann, joined the National Guard.

Karl Hermann's father died in 1848. To escape the political unrest in Baden, Karl went to St. Gallen in Switzerland and then worked as secretary in the noted Hotel Feder in Genora, Italy. Here he met some *L Genoa* young officers of the American navy and visited their ship. He decided to go to America. His brother Johann was already in the United States.

Karl Hermann left his home in Heidelberg Feb. 12, 1853. He took passage on the sailing ship St.Denis at Havre on Feb. 23. The passage took 43 days. He celebrated his 27th birthday during a terrific storm on March 11. He landed at New York on April 4.

He took a train to the end of the railroad at Pittsburgh, where he took an Ohio River steamer to Cairo on the Mississippi. He changed boats again at Napoleon at the mouth of the Arkansas River. The trip from Pittsburgh to Napoleon took eight days. It required an entire day to cross the Mississippi overflow. The shores were dotted with the cabins of squatters who furnished firewood for the boats.

After eight days, above Little Rock, the water became lower and lower, and the boat had to be cordelled over sandbars, while the passengers, spent hours on shore, hunting game. When near ~~Dardanelle~~ the boat *L Dardanella* stuck on a sandbar and the captain gave up the attempt to get it loose and decided to await the next high water freshet. Ten passengers, including Karl Hermann, then decided to walk to the nearest plantation and secure passage on a wagon to the nearest town. They finally reached the highway and 18 hours later arrived in VanBuren, on May 8, 1853.

Karl Hermann at once went to the settlement of Hermannsburg in Washington County, 1½ miles from the Indian Territory and 40 miles north of Fort Smith. Here his brother Johann and a friend had buried themselves in the forest to hunt game and live an idyllic existence. He found his brother's house still incomplete. He met his brother's wife Nani and their newly-born daughter Eliese.

(He then tells about the characters who congregated around the mill, rural customs, etc., and describes the attention that a stranger attracted in this isolated place.)

In September 1853, Karl drove with his brother's family for a visit with her people in Franklin County, Missouri, where the Missouri Pacific railroad was just ~~building~~ [builded] through the Wilhelmi farm. He remained with the Wilhelmi family five weeks and became engaged to the daughter of the house, sister to Nani, his brother's wife. Her father then agreed to move with them to Arkansas as soon as Karl could build a home for his future wife.

In November he and his brother and family reached Arkansas and made preparations for building a house and a store. In February Karl went back to Missouri to visit his betrothed. September 2 was agreed on as the wedding day and preparations were made for the moving to Arkansas, his father-in-law, the latter's son Julius and family to accompany them. But it was October before the party left, with four wagons and eight horses. The trunks were sent by boat to VanBuren, Ark., but did not arrive until 18 months later, and the linen and clothing they contained had spoiled.

Twenty-one days later they reached Hermannsburg. They spent the winter building a house and a store. The following February Karl went to New York to buy supplies for his store. He then went to New Orleans and on the return, low water kept them for three months, but finally he reached home, shortly before the birth of his first child.

The goods he had purchased were to follow on the next ship but the river got too low and remained low during the entire summer of 1855, so that his goods bought in New York and household furniture bought in Cincinnati did not arrive. These goods remained at the mouth of the Arkansas River, exposed to all sorts of dangers not covered by insurance. So Karl made tables, chairs and bed. The Hermanns did without such necessities as salt and ink. The high water of the following February made it possible to secure the goods and furniture that hadn't spoiled or become lost.

Because of the great distance from cities of trade and the difficulty of overland transport from the north, he was confined to once-a-year purchase of supplies, by the short season of river transport. He learned about the purchase and sale of sugar and coffee, dry goods, medicine and books, vinegar and molasses, shoes and hats, glassware and china, salt, tools, knives and forks, saddles, plows, etc.

In February of the following year, when his son Edward was only two weeks old, he began another business trip. In New Orleans he met his Hermannsburg neighbor, Dannenberg, who told him that his wife was seriously ill. He took passage on the steamer Forrest City but he was delayed and the steamer left without him, only to explode her boiler and kill many passengers. Two weeks were consumed on the river trip from Napoleon to Van Buren. Meanwhile the goods purchased in the east were destroyed when the Ohio River steamboat burned, only the piano being saved.

Karl Hermann's home at Hermannsburg stood on a hill, with the vegetable garden in front of it. Steps were cut into stone to reach the house. Across the street was his brother John's home, with the hills behind it. In the valley below was the Hermanns' store, farther on across the road, the mill. North on a third hill lived his brother-in-law Julius. On either side of Karl's house lived his neighbors, Kraft and Schmidt.

Karl Hermann bought a slave named Melinda for $950 in gold, who soon learned to speak German. It was seven miles to the nearest doctor and there was no drug store anywhere. Because of the nearness to Indian Territory, care had to be taken that the Cherokees did not get spirituous liquors from the Hermanns' store. But the Cherokees were good friends with the Germans, because they thought they were a race similar to themselves and they knew that the Germans were not the same as the other settlers of those parts.

In 1860 delegates were elected to a convention in Little Rock to decide if Arkansas were to secede or remain in the Union. The vote in this district was held in the seven-miles-distant Boonsboro, better known as Cane Hill, and the Secessionists were victorious.

When it became evident that civil war was unavoidable, Karl began, on advice of his brother John, to bury his coin. His neighbors, Legg and Dannenberg, also brought their money to him to care for, which later caused much unpleasantness. Metal coin disappeared from circulation and Confederate paper money took its place. In place of small change, merchants printed paper currency.

Because of the exposed position between North and South, this section suffered more than most from the activities of bushwhackers after the battle of Wilson's Creek. Hermannsburg was between two armies and two fires. Bushwhackers carried on pillage and robbery under the flag of both sides, now robbing as Federals and now parading as Confederates. Many prominent Secessionists, including Governor Jackson of Missouri, stopped overnight at the Hermann home on their flight to Texas. Slaves in northwest Arkansas fled to Kansas, and Melinda, the Hermanns' slave, also disappeared with her child.

— H —

(Editor's note: We interrupt the Hermannsburg story here, in order to record some previously unpublished letters from Johann Hermann to his mother in Germany. The first letter is from LeHavre, France, written on 28 July 1849. A month later he was able to write from New York (exclamation point). The last letter in this series was written by Nanni, dated 22 September 1852, giving first impressions of Hermannsburg, Washington County, Arkansas. — WJL)

— H —

EXCERPTS FROM LETTERS
WRITTEN BY JOHANN HERMANN AND HIS WIFE NANNY

Le Havre, 28 July 1849
Dear Mother:

   Just a few words to tell you of my safe arrival here. In Basel I was delayed a day because of my French passport. I arrived in Paris yesterday evening. When I learned that the ship would sail on the 29th, I had to leave Paris that same evening by train, arriving here at 6 o'clock in the morning. All day I was busy getting ready for my departure tomorrow at 4 o'clock on the ship Louisiana. I found a letter from Wilhelm (his brother) with enclosure from H. Muench for his brother.

   Again thanks, dear Mother, for the loving care you devoted to me. I will always think of you with deep respect and love. Take care of yourselves, all of you, and hope for an early safe Wiedersehen. Adieu, Adieu!

                              Your loving son Jean Hermann
                      — H ——

New York, 31 August 1849.
Dear Mother!

   You have received my letter from Havre and noted that I arrived there safely. But you are probably waiting more anxiously for this letter, to assure you that I made my ocean voyage successfully. On the 26th of this month I set foot on American soil, in good health and pleased with the completion of the voyage.

   From earlier reports I knew that New York is a fine city but I could not have imagined its real magnificence. But I cannot remain here. According to all those to whom I was recommended, it is not possible for a foreigner to get a position as an engineer or draftsman immediately. I must first work some time as a laborer and then climb up to the engineer's rung. But the large number of immigrants, many of whom came without means and cannot travel farther, have caused an overcrowding, and they must get a loan to go farther into the country.

   I have therefore decided to leave tonight via Albany to Buffalo and from there cross Lake Erie and go to Detroit. If I cannot find a suitable position in Michigan, then I will be on the way to St.Louis. I do not know where I will be, so cannot give you an address. In a few weeks I should be certain and will then write you a detailed letter.

   The information that follows is for Karl (his younger brother) or others who plan to make the trip. Of food supplies, take ham, butter and the like from home. Lay in other supplies at Havre, especially potatoes, bread, etc. Buy from Mme. Leroux, rues Dauphine et de la Crique No. 7. Buy nothing in the storeroom of the shipping company. If one starts the trip in the season when there are few storms, that is from May to August, then I think the following food supplies will be sufficient: 25 lbs of white hardtack, potatoes, new beans from home 2 pounds, peas 2 pounds, dried fruit 2 pounds, rice 4 pounds, flour 3 pounds, salted butter 4 pounds, a well-smoked ham of about 10 pounds, salt 1½ to 2 pounds, vinegar 2 liter, wine only a few bottles or a small jug, brandy 3 liter, ground coffee 1 pound, chocolate 1 pound, tea ¼ pound, sugar 5-6 pounds, a jar of cooking oil, pepper, cinnamon,

22

THE WILHELMIS

WILHELM WILHELMI

1887.

LINA WILHELMI
married Karl Hermann

NANNI WILHELMI
married Johann Hermann

onions, eggs 30, citron 12 pieces. Everything to be packed in sausage casings, especially the butter, flour, salt and coffee.

The following utensils are necessary: a water-bottle with a wide mouth, a tin wash basin, also tin plates, small bowl, cooking pot, drinking glass, knife, fork, spoon, a night chamber with cover of zinc, and a few medicines such as laxative pills, Hoffmans-drops, and a few others. These things, together with a bit of courage and as few big expectations as possible should bring anyone across in 30 days, with moderate weather.

If you travel in the middle deck, choose if possible a place for the bed in the middle of the ship, because there the roll of the ship is not so severe and because there is an opening nearby through which fresh air can come in. Don't forget a few ropes and nails, with which to tie up the boxes. Also do not forget to haggle with the agency. If they ask 50 fr., you can beat him down 20-25 fr., especially if there are other ships in harbor for this same trip.

When you arrive here and have the company of others who plan to go to the same hotel, hire a horse and wagon, which costs 2 fl 30 kr, and be sure that while your effects are being unloaded from the ship, also enroute to the hotel, someone is there to watch. Then you climb proud-ly into the wagon and drive to the Hotel Shakespeare, where the rates are 4 dollars per week or .75 per day. Good also is the Swiss Hall on Greenwich street a 1/3 dollar.

Time presses me. It is already 2 o'clock and I leave at 6, yet must go all over town to pick up some letters of recommendation. I greet and kiss all of you.

Your loving son Hannes
— H —

New Port (Mo.), 4 November 1849
Dear Mother:
My winter quarters are settled and I am now in a position to send you my address, in the hope of hearing from you. You will have re-ceived my letter from New York. I will now tell you of my travel since then. After I had looked around New York and had delivered my letters of recommendation, none of which was of any use to me, I went up the Hudson via steamboat to Albany; from there by train to Buffalo, then by steamboat to Detroit; then again by train to New-Buffalo, from where a steamboat brought me to Chicago. Here I took a canal boat to LaSalle and then again a steamboat on the Illinois River to the Miss-issippi and St. Louis.

L Heddaeus

Here I stayed eight days, during which I delivered my letters of recommendation but they were of no more use than in New York. But accidentally I met /Heddaus von Heidelberg and Wilhelmi von Offenburg, the latter my room-mate in Karlsruhe at the Widow Schneeberger's. Wilhelmi wants to buy land, because his parents want to come next spring. We knew the Missouri valley to be a healthy and fruitful place. Also, I had two letters for that area. So we decided to make a trip on foot. Our expectations were surpassed in the area between New-Port and Hermann. Here, and only an English mile from New-Port, lives Muench, *L friend* brother of the Lyoner Muench, /Frienc of Wilhelm, (Johann's brother in Lyon). I had a letter addressed to him and was so hospitably received that I decided to spend the winter with him. Muench is a farmer, not married, and a very active man. I share all work, for which I get board and room. But what is best, I have the opportunity to learn the speech and customs of the Americans. By spring I hope to be able to make my way anywhere.

If Karl (his younger brother) still has a desire to come here, he should learn the English language as much as he can.

I see by the newspapers that the Cholera broke out in Mannheim. I worry about Amalie (his sister). Last summer this sickness took many lives here but has now completely disappeared.

Now I will give Karl some advice in case he comes here. Instead of a big chest, he should have two smaller ones made. It makes it easier to pack and unpack, which he will have to do himself. Then he should never let his possessions out of his sight. Don't drag along too many clothes and don't put any money in the chests -- it causes worry. He can make the journey over here as I made it but he should not let himself be induced to buy tickets for longer distances than New York to Albany, Buffalo, Detroit, Chicago, LaSalle, St.Louis. Never deal with outsiders, but after he has learned the price, have his things brought on board the ship. Here, during the trip, his money will be demanded and for which he will receive a card. The cost of steamboat travel varies from day to day, according to the number of departing steamers.

To Albany he can travel second class, as the trip is only 12 hours, but he must take some food along. From there, the emigrant train to Buffalo. In short, he can travel to Chicago 2nd class but must always take food along. From Chicago he takes the Post-Canal ship. If I am still here at that time, he should store his chests in the hotel and only take necessities with him, via the boat, Lake of the Woods, to Washington, Franklin County (Mo.), from where he can come to me on foot exactly 8 English miles.

However, if I should no longer be here, he will find in the post-office in St. Louis a letter from me, which will tell him my present abode. As the best time to travel, I recommend the month of July, so that he will arrive here about the middle of August or early September. Earlier than that, the heat is such that he is not accustomed to it. If he comes through Paris, he should get me two Rechenschieber, one of 26 and one of 36 cm. length, from Lenoir. Any optician can tell him where he lives. If Karl can pack his kitchen utensils, which he must buy in Havre, in his chest, he should not sell it in New York but take it with him.

The trip cost me to St.Louis, with all, nearly 400 fl; 600 fl I deposited in a solid house in St. Louis to which I was /recomennded from *[recommended]* Lyon by Angelroot, Egers and Barth, and 400 fl. for emergency in the Equally good bank in Washington. *[equally]*

So, dear Mother, I am eager to hear from you as soon as possible and I am counting the days till I get the lucky and good news from home, from Uncle Johann (his mother's brother), /Mathilde (his sister), *[Mathilde]* Amalie and all the other loved ones. Greetings to all from your faithful son.

                                        Jean Hermann

Memphis, 20 March 1850
Dear Mother:

Just to give you a sign of life from me, I am writing these lines, for I have little of interest to relate. From my stop with Muench and my employment there, you are already informed. At the end of November came ~~Ilhelmi~~, son of the Reverend Wilhelmi of Bauschlott by Pforzheim, to me, and begged me to follow him to his newly purchased farm, to help him in the building and installations. He bought the farm in the name of his parents, who will come over this year. I accepted his offer, since it made my position more pleasant and since I could perfect myself in necessary projects.

L Wilhelmi

Finally, at the beginning of February, I received your long awaited letter, which reported on you and the others. I used the address of Ganter (college classmate of Johann at Heidelberg) immediately made the tip to the 30-hour distant place, where I found him. From that time we discussed the best thing to do. Bad weather has only now left us carry out our plans. At this moment, we are on a steamboat bound for Tennessee and Arkansas, from which we have had good accounts.

You will probably ask "What are you going to do there? And in spite of my warning that you can't succeed by yourself." But, dear Mother, here it is not like over there. Here one becomes laborer, master, and again laborer, often in one month; where a man in the moment when he can earn the most will alter not only his position but even his occupation. A shoemaker here also operates a confectionery and a hotel, and if he can sell them tomorrow at a profit, he will do it and become baker, butcher or farmer whichever he considers most profitable. He can always sell, for nothing is overcrowded. You see, by accepting a job I am not bound, which is what you fear.

Also, I see here that I am not as young as you like to think. Here I am an "old bachelor" and if being an old bachelor is a disadvantage, it is here. The American marries at 20-22 years and presents a fine front for his family. All unmarried immigrants are nobodies. So you see that, even in this regard, your wish cannot come true. Even rich American women get no dower from their parents, and although I do not demand much, I want at least something from her side to help and ease my lot. I therefore make you this proposition, which Ganter's sister also made, that someone find me a wife. My chief qualifications are these, and they are hard to find: A girl must be able to run a household, be healthy, and dare not have too much so-called culture. As for the European emphasis on birth, I see absolutely nothing.

A way of life as I have described it will be easy for you to attain, if you try to make some acquaintances in the city or country. I would come back about November and straighten out the matter. Then on our return in the spring we would find everything here prepared for us. So, dear Mother, risk a chance on my wheel of fortune, without being disturbed all night long by fear, doubt and things that might happen.

In my last letter I purposely refrained from asking for political news because I shudder when I think of such, and I can assure you that the chief reason for my worry is that persons dear to me face such a dark and tragic future. It is not possible that Europe in this condition can last long and it is certain that conditions can be changed

only through terrible power struggles. Therefore my advice is the same
as last year, which few believed: Every one who does not feel called
on to sacrifice his property and life for one party or another, there
is still time, in this portion of false peace, and better now than
later with much greater loss.

You, dear Mother, are risking your property won by hard work and
are risking the lives of two sons. Think this over. I can only tell
you — and it is my duty to tell you — that the foregoing is my own
belief and that of many others.

The Cholera had declined by the time I got here and the epidemic was
never as serious as described in the newspapers. St.Louis, in spite of
fire and Cholera is big and beautiful — more beautiful than formerly.
All in all I am well pleased here and I am convinced it will please
everyone who can throw off the European plunder.

Your next letter, in which I hope to learn more about conditions
over there, and which I am eagerly anticipating, should be addressed
in Ganter's name, since in this way the letters are sure to reach me.
Do not fear that any secrets in your letter will be violated by him.
For — for the money that Eduard (his youngest brother) must sacrifice for
the Prussian shooting affairs, he could have made a wonderful trip to
the United States of America, without any danger that during a street
riot he might get hit on the head with a rock or something else. Of
course he would have had to give up his German citizenship and face
the prospect of going hungry. Dear Mother, what I write is irony, so
don't feel bad about it; I mean it well.

And now, in conclusion, like the end of all songs, the request that
in case our present means are not sufficient, you arrange affairs so
that something be held for us. I cannot give an exact sum but I think
1500 fl. would be enough to reach my goal.

To you and all the others, hearty greetings. I remain your true and
thankful son

                              Hannes Hermann

PS: Write, dear Mother, on every address to me: By steamer via
Liverpool.
                        —— H ——

Freyschlags-Farm, 21 June 1850
(Washington County, Arkansas)

Dear Good Mother!

I was sorry to read in your letter of 24 April which came yesterday
that you had suffered a fall on the ice, but I am of the opinion that
Baden-Baden will fix you up.

You suggest two girls for me: The Wilhelmi sister and a girl named
Steppbecher. I am only 350 miles distant from the first one, but 1500
miles from the second one. I feel like making the 350 mile trip as
soon as I can get away here. Nothing could be easier. I do not need a
passport and not much baggage. A pair of pants, 2 shirts, 2 pair sox

and 2 handkerchiefs will be fastened on my horse and I can get there in 10 or 12 days. Expenses will be about 1 fl.15 kr. per day but will not cover the necessary purchase of tools and wagon and horses. All of these are considerably cheaper in St.Louis than here, so I'll save 30-35 Fl. on each horse, 5o fl. on the wagon, and so on. My trunks are still at Wilhelmi's. It would cost at least 15 Fl. if I had these shipped by freight.

If the girl pleases me, she will be placed on top of all the things in the wagon, along with cooking/untensils, food, bed and a tent. We will drive 20 miles each day, build a fire at night and sleep until daybreak. That is the way that thousands of people each year are traveling to California, Oregon, Texas, etc. and they are often 7 months on the way.

[margin note left: L utensils]

But you do not know where I really will drive with my tender wife. Always southwest from St. Louis, to the northwest corner of the state of Arkansas. You may wonder why I am settling so deep in the wilderness and so far from civilization. You may even fear that the Indians, who are only an hour's ride from my home, might eat me up. In our area they are not considered dangerous or as pictured in the lying German newspapers. At this frontier of civilization there lives a peaceful but brave people, blessed with pure republican virtues. People are not crowded together as they are in Germany or even in the eastern states of America. The country is inhabited and only where the land is poor need one ride 15 or 20 miles to a neighbor. There are no bands of robbers, as is often the case in Germany, not even a police force. Who handles law and order? The people themselves. They are happy and every one makes a living. Every citizen, because of his own personal interests, is a custodian of law and order. A robber could not get 20 miles without being caught and hung. Word travels like fire; a farmer rides to his neighbor with the report and usually with the identification of the culprit. Where there are so few people, everyone knows friends and strangers. And through the American talent for prompt action and sharp memory, the culprit is known at once. You simply have to find out who is missing. I am often surprised to hear that children of 10-12 years, can describe a missing horse which they had seen from their home for only a few minutes. (Horses have free range in the forest around here and often have no stable.)

At this moment I am living at the mill of an old German named Frey-schlag von Karrback (Rheinbaiern), former owner of the ferry at Mannheim, a brave and well-to-do man. All of his daughters with one exception are unmarried; the youngest is a new bride. His son Hermann will be married next week; his daughters Babett, Meta, Christina, and sons Eduard and Heinrich, went to California last year ('49 Gold Rush) and according to their reports they are getting along well in the diggings. They made the journey, about 2400 English miles, mostly on/feer and L foot were 7 months on the way. Their horses and cattle died on the journey or were killed by Indians. These, however, are different Indian tribes than those who live here on the Arkansas border.

[margin note left: L Karrbach]

As for the money for which I asked you, I would like to have it this year, so as not to lose another year. I wish you would send me as much as you can and if it is the entire remainder of my inheritance from my father, so much the better. Although it is easy to borrow money here, yet the interest rate of 10 per cent is damn high, and any purchase in cash gives the buyer an advantage.

29

I have not yet told you what persuaded me to settle here. We have excellent soil and a fine climate, better than Missouri. Winter lasts only 6 weeks to 2 months, during which the cattle can always find pasture. And the thing on which I have set my eye, the silk industry. I have found a farm that I can buy, which has fine water-power, good buildings, excellent soil and drinking water, as well as location. The water-power gives me the opportunity of spinning silk and obtaining the best price. Wine also brings a high price, so the Hermanns' wine will sell for 2 dollars(5 fl.) per gallon. One man, whose acquaintance I made, made 1700 from one acre. I myself was in Hermann (Mo.) and convinced myself. The Americans do not understand vineyards and wine-making; only the Germans have experimented here. Several Americans asked me just how wine was made, if the grapes were cooked! Also, they lack the patience.

If nothing comes of my project with Miss Wilhelmi, then I will ride back here, with my trunks; wait till I have everything in order; and then leave here for Germany in October. By that time the money should be here and I can buy the place. Ganter can run the household until I return. I can assure you, dear Mother, that in this free fresh life, where every man recognizes every other man as an individual, and where the senseless rank- and blood-differences do not count, that I have thawed out and feel well, especially when I wander all day long in these great woods and never get tired but always admire the greatness and magnificence of Nature.

I have covered a considerable distance -- about 2800 English miles by steam, 500 on foot, and about 300 on horseback. I just happened to remember that this letter has to get to the postoffice, 9 miles from here. All kind regards, dear Mother, and greetings to all from your

faithful/~~John~~ Hannes L son

— H —

Freyschlags-Mill, 10 July 1850

Dear Brother: (His brother Wilhelm who had worked in a bank in Lyon, France, since 1823.)

For a long time I have intended writing to you but I am living from day to day in expectation of fixing my permanent abode, so have postponed writing to you who has had such a large part in my fate. I wanted to be able to write you something definite about my future. But I won't wait any longer but will tell you about my experiences and my plans for the future.

At present I am busy learning the language, customs and country and think I am now far enough advanced to stand on my own feet. As long as I was in Missouri I had the plan of opening a mine, of which there are many, iron, copper, lead and some silver. But I soon saw that greater capital would be needed than I could raise and that the greatest difficulty would be the poor roads to the markets. Farming brings only a comfortable existence and is tied up with too much hard work and too many things one has to do without. So that farming, for one who was not brought up on a farm, is difficult. Part of the blame rests on the poor wages paid for farm work.

Since life in the country pleases me better than life in town, I thought of something that I could produce in small quantities and could start on a small scale. I thought of wine and silk cultivation. I studied the wine industry in Missouri — Hermann, where most residents are Germans engaged in the wine business and have had excellent results for the past 4 years. On the average they produce 550 gallons on one acre of land. A gallon costs 2 dollars here but in the larger cities like St. Louis, New Orleans, etc. 12 bottles cost 10 dollars. In St. Louis the price on the restaurant cards was given as 2 dollars per bottle. Naturally I got to thinking and I thought I knew as much about the wine industry as the shoemaker Deubner in Hermann, who last year made 1700 dollars on one acre and had no vineyard experience. The town of Hermann did not please me. The winters are too cold and in the spring there are often night-frosts which would hurt any silk industry.

So, with Ganter I got on the road south and after several weeks and 1100 English miles by train and 400 miles on foot, I arrived in Washington County, Arkansas, where I found all the things I desired: rich upland soil, springs and brooks in great numbers, and a healthy location as proved by the appearance of the inhabitants. In the river valleys are grape vines a foot thick, climbing up as high on oak trees as 100 feet. These grapes, however, ripen in the winter; others with larger berries cover entire hills. The spring here, like the winter, is mild, and the summer not too hot; this is fine for silk culture.

Among other places for sale, one pleased me especially — 160 acres, good buildings, spring, a brook for power, and a healthy location. The water-power makes the place valuable, because I want to spin the silk from the cocoons. There are several in this area who are engaged in the silk industry and if my little spinning mill is successful, it will help me a lot. The price of a bushel of cocoons is 2 dollars, from which more than a pound of silk can be produced, and a pound of the silk is worth 4 dollars.

Even when I was still in Europe I got interested in the silk industry and I would like to have a book on silk and how it is produced and dyed etc. Can you send me such a book, since you are familiar with the producing business?

For the past two months I have been living with a German named Freyschlag, former owner of the Sandhofer ferry. His children were raised in Mannheim and know Elise and Amalie (two sisters of Johann) personally. Herr Freyschlag has a mill, which I repaired for him and to which I made several additions and improvements. In a few weeks I will erect a cotton gin about 12 english miles from here and will manage the gin and mill there, since the owner is away from home. I receive 40 dollars per month and board and room for me and my horse. When I add that I have always been healthy and happy and am now going around with thoughts of marriage in my head, you know all - everything that I know about myself.

Johann

--- H ---

31

Port Williams, 12 October 1850

Dear good Mother!

I have been back from Arkansas for about 3 weeks and have moved into
my former winter quarters for a short time. Until today I could not
tell you anything definite. / ~~My wishes are always way ahead of every~~
~~thing.~~ However, I will do my best to reach my goal. As regards my settlement, things have changed. The son of Freyschlag also got the California fever, along with his father and two sisters, and now seeks to
sell his mill, which I, if the price and terms are acceptable, will
buy. I have run this mill by myself for the past three months and am
convinced that by diligent work, it will be a big success. Tomorrow on
Sunday I will visit Ganter, to consult with him and to see if he has
any desire to be my partner in buying the mill. In any case, I will
return to Arkansas this fall — at least that is my plan. In my next
letter, which should follow closely on this one, if nothing unexpected
happens I hope to write you something definite. I have to decide, because I have had enough of this homeless wandering-about.

You, dear Mother, you will be unpleasantly moved by my decision to
settle here. It is the only solution, but I have not given up the hope
of visiting you in a short time. This is my sincere wish, and is certain if Ganter joins me, as seems certain. Karl's plan to come here
makes me glad. But he must have no illusions. Here he must work at
everything, and although damaged, he will be a free man who does what
he does for himself. If he wants to learn to work, the carpenters,
cabinet makers, wagon makers, or blacksmiths are much in demand. Then
next spring, in April or May, he can travel via New Orleans.

> Greetings to all from
> Your loving son Hannes Hermann
> ——— H ———

Port William, 24 October 1850

Dear Good Mother!

A few days ago I received your letter, handed to me by Ganter. I am
glad to hear that you are well.

According to the plans which you already know, I have returned to
the Wilhelmi family where I found two lovely daughters. After a three
weeks stay, I could no longer refrain from telling my chosen one that
I am in love with her. I cannot describe my joy when she said Yes. In
my dear Nanni I have full assurance that she is a well-trained house-
keeper who will bring my happiness in the future. Consequently, my
journey to see you must be postponed, but not given up. I regret that
the anticipation of seeing you again was premature, and ask you now to
give me your approval and blessing in writing, if not in person.

From my last letter from Arkansas you know that, with the exception
of Hermann Freyschlag, the rest of the family have gone to California.
Hermann also talks of making the California trip. Nothing could be
luckier for me, because if the mill is for sale, I know its possibili-
ties through experience and have learned the real profits that can be
made and more safely than in other occupations.

L. Freyking suits my wishes.

The wishes of my future parents-in-law are that I should settle here if possible. I agreed provided that I was offered the same opportunity here as in Arkansas, which I doubt.

Your worry about the safety and cost of sending the money is unnecessary. I will probably lose this winter in Arkansas and it is just this winter that the United States will pay an old debt to the Indians of 1,700,000 dollars and all of this money will come to Arkansas. Freyschlag could then raise the price of his mill or change his mind altogether.

Anyway, I am closer to you in Arkansas than in St.Louis, for I can make the journey to New Orleans via the Arkansas and Mississippi Rivers in 6 to 8 days, and the journey from St.Louis to New York would cost twice as much in time and money. Hearty greetings to all from your son

Hannes
— H —

24 October 1850
Honored Lady!

From the letters of your dear son, my beloved bridegroom, you will have felt that I am fortunate to be his bride, and only your trust in me and adoption as your daughter are lacking to make my happiness complete. If I could tell you in person how much I honor you and how much I love your dear son, I would assure you that I will do all in my power to make him happy. And if it should ever be my good fortune to see you face to face, then I will thank you in person and assure you that I will be an obedient daughter.

Please give all your dear ones, greetings from their unknown new member of the family. My dear parents and brothers and sisters ask me to tell you of their friendship and respect. Much happiness to you! I close with deep respect, if you permit it.

Your devoted daughter, Nanny Wilhelmi
— H —

Port William, November 1850
Dear Mother!

As I recall, in my last letter I forgot to tell you that until further notice, all letters addressed to me at my last winter's address are correct. Ganter has returned to Arkansas, where he may conclude the purchase (of the mill) this winter.

My bride sends her greetings and asks that you accept her as a daughter, which I do not doubt you would do if you knew this angel. Best greetings to all, especially dear Uncle Johann (brother of his mother) from

Your loving son Hannes,
care of Mr.Wilhelmi, Port William, Franklin Co., Mo.,
America, by steamer via Liverpool

— H —

My dear good Mother!

I read your last letter with deep feeling and inner pleasure. On 27 April came my beloved Hermann hale and hearty. Right now he sits beside me and kisses me every instant and disturbs my writing. Isn't he naughty?

Last Tuesday, May 13, we were married, first by my dear father in a church ceremony and then a short ceremony by a Justice of the Peace, according to local custom. How much we though of you in these hectic days, our beloved but distant Mother, and wished that you could be with us. We decided to write you on that very day, but it was impossible, because our horses, already saddled, were in the yard, on which we rode 12 miles to nearby Washington (Mo.). There we hunted up some old friends and after three days we returned here.

Day after tomorrow we will transact business in St.Louis and then the great journey, 350 miles by wagon, to our new home will begin. Although it hurts to leave my dear parents and others, but I am glad to travel far away with my good Man. From this, beloved Mother, you can see how happy I am that your son possesses me. I will do everything possible to make him happy. To see you, dear Mother, and prove my affection by deed, is my greatest wish. To that end I will gladly risk all dangers which such a long journey entails -- I know from experience - and if it is possible some time, with my Hans, to visit you.

My thanks for the handsome wedding gift. As soon as we are in our little home in Arkansas, I will send you a detailed description of our life and doings there , so that you can join us in spirit. Also, I ask that you let us hear from you soon, how things are going because we have a deep interest in your well-being. I do not have to assure you of this.

Please give our greetings to all relations. My folks greet yours. In my thoughts I kiss you dearly.
Your obedient thankful daughter Nanny Hermann
the 18 May 1851
--- H ---

Port Williams, 19 May 1851

Dearly beloved Mother!
You will be mad at me because I haven't answered your last letter of 25 December, which I received in March. But since that time I had so much to do. During that time I had to travel to Arkansas, find a good mill, and buy a house with kitchen, stable, etc. And then ride back (360 miles) to FortWilliam and get married. Isn't that enough activity to make letter-writing superfluous? But finally, I am at this point.

Tomorrow, with my dear little wife and one laborer, who also wants to go to Arkansas, I will drive to St.Louis, to cash a check and buy various things for our home. We will return in 8 or 9 days and then will embark on the great journey in a four-horse wagon, on which my wife and chests will have to keep each other company for 18 to 20 days, during which I will ride the saddle-horse and do the driving.

If I remember correctly, I have pictured this journey in earlier letters from Arkansas; I mean/prophecised. You see that a good lawyer *[prophesied]* went lost when I came over. I bought a mill, which five years earlier had been built by a certain B. Smith, but lack of funds and too many debts, he never finished it and it was sold at public auction. After that, the mill was in several hands, none of whom was able to bring the mill in operation because B. Smith's employees went to court and secured a lien on the mill. I went to the Clerk's office, where the records are open to anyone, and learned that since the 13 April 1846 no further complaint from the employees had been entered. According to the local authorities, such a complaint is dead after 5 years, which the former owner evidently did not know. So, after the 13 April, I could buy without any risk.

The mill, as I have said, is not finished. The mill-race has to be dug and several stone structures have to be built and other minor things, which will cost me work and money. However, it is a desirable location in every respect, in the center of a rich section of Arkansas, on the Texas road, and with a more constant water-flow than any other mill. I had to pay 900 dollars for it, which may seem high to you for an unfinished structure. But this mill will be worth much more to me than Freyschlag's mill and has other advantages. Hermann Freyschlag asked 5000 dollars for his mill and inventory. I think I can finish my mill with an expenditure of 1200 dollars. This is more than I have in *[capital]* ~~captal~~, in case Ganter, who has half-and-half, goes to Oregon next spring (2400 miles).

In this case I would have to borrow money, which would be unpleasant at the high interest rate (8 to 10 %). Old Mr. Freyschlag died shortly after my departure from Arkansas last fall. His two still single daughters have gone to California to be with their brothers and sisters.

So, as you begin to read this letter, we have been married for one week. We are both very happy and are confident that our happiness will continue. We have often thought of you, dear Mother, and wished that you were near and could join in our happiness. My dear Nanni thinks constantly of the possibility of visiting you some time, which we will do if nothing unforeseen prevents. My thanks, dear Mother, for the prompt and liberal sending of money and for the lovely gift for my sweetheart, also thanks for the congratulations of my sisters and brothers, to whom I will write as soon as I can.

Ganter asks you, through me, to buy a gun from the gunmaker Bauern-feind, where I bought my guns, a gun of this quality: Barrell 90 French cm long, about 50 shot per pound, with powder and two flints. Ganter also wants a six-shot revolver that will fire about 50 shot per pound, with easy trigger and which is loaded from the front, not from the back. You can probably buy such pistols ready-made. So if you have a chance to send these either to St. Louis or New Orleans, it would please Ganter very much. He will, of course, also use his own efforts to obtain them. He will repay any transportation charges. His order convinces me that he is willing to go to Oregon, because here we have no use for such murder instruments. I will finish this letter in St. Louis. For today, Adieu, dear Mother.

(Postscript on next page.)

Belleville, 26 May 1851

I got the money from the St. Louis banker and am sending you the re-
ceipt for my inheritance from my father, with thanks for your prompt-
ness. I have one more request, dear Mother, and this is the first time
I have asked it. I would like to have a really valuable decoration in
my home, and that is a photograph of you. So I beg that you will have
your picture taken and send it to me by any means available. If the
art of photography had come this far, I would already have had a picture made of my little wife. Daguerreotypes are made here but I do not
like them -- they are so dark and seldom good.
    Hearty greetings to all of you from your loving son,
                          John Hermann
                          by steamer via Liverpool,
                          Boonsboro P.O., Washington County,
                          North America, Arkansas
                          --- H ---

Washington County, 15 July 1851
Dear Mother!

About three weeks ago we arrived here safe and sound -- my wife, a
German workman from Hornberg named George Hackinjos, and myself. Our
journey was quite an adventure, so I'll write a short account of it.
After I had bought at Port William four horses and a wagon and had
made the harness myself, we drove to St. Louis and Belleville to buy
things necessary for the equipment of the mill and our new home.

    Immediately after our return from St. Louis, we began our long trip.
We had secured some kitchen utensils and foodstuffs, so that we could
prepare a noonday meal, while the horses rested and grazed. On the
second day we found it much more pleasant to camp in the open than to
spend the night in houses where the heat and sometimes lice disturbed
our sleep. So we stopped sometime before sundown where there was good
water and grass for the horses. I put up the tent and built a fire,
while George took care of the horses and made his bed under the wagon.
Then I would buy eggs and milk at some nearby farmhouse -- we had our
own ham, bacon and meal -- from which my lady prepared a supper to
gladden the heart. We would talk for a while and then go to bed. At
2 o'clock in the morning, poor old George finally was able to wake me
up. He also had slept soundly and noticed too late that a terrific
thunderstorm was directly over us. The thunder had not been able to
wake us from our sound sleep.

    I built up the fire, took the tent to cover the wagon, my wife hast-
ily cooked coffee, baked cornbread and fried bacon, then we hitched up
the horses. It was pitch dark and only our little fire and the lightning gave us illumination for our work. Just when everything was done,
the rain came down in torrents but we sat in the wagon and ate our
meal. I hoped that the rain would stop at daybreak, but not so. The
sky was overcast with dark clouds and left us little hope that we
could wait for better weather. So we drove to the first house, where
we waited till mid-afternoon for better weather. We then resumed our
journey. The next night a heavy rain forced us to spend a night in
a house. The next night and the following nights were beautiful, and
from then on, with the exception of two nights, we camped in the open.
On the 15th day we arrived here.

I found many things to do before we could begin work on the mill. I had to establish my entire household — buy cows, pigs, fodder and bring them home, also to thresh and haul to the mill the wheat that Ganter had harvested, so that we could have flour in the house. In short, there were many things to do and many expenditures. Of the 1400 dollars, which, as you know from my last letter, I received in St. Louis, I have spent: For the mill 900 dollars, for 3 horses 195 dollars, wagon 70 dollars, for construction on the mill 85 dollars, for the household about 80 dollars. I still need to buy lumber and labor, which will cost at least 300 dollars.

As you can see from the above account, my money is nearer the bottom than the top of the cash register and it is certain that I will have to borrow. Will you, dear Mother, loan me the 1600 fl. that you were willing to give me, with a good mortgage at 5 %, I will accept the loan with thanks. It is certain that as soon as my mill is in operation, money will come in just as fast as it is now going out. And I will not be delinquent with the interest payments. I could borrow the money here but would have to pay 10 % interest. And I do not like the idea of losing everything I have for a debt of 400 to 500 dollars.

The laws here are good but the heads only good enough to circumvent the best laws. This mill was sold five years ago at a public sale for 50 dollars, while three other creditors were there who had loaned the mill 1900 dollars. You can therefore see why I distrust the local creditors and must not incur any debts. From the above you will also see that the mill and everything belonging to it is my personal property and that I have not formed a partnership with Ganter. Ganter is restless and wants to go farther west, to California or Oregon, probably in the spring. He is not interested in the mill except that he loaned me 300 dollars at 6 % interest. This I will have to pay him by January.

I repeat my earlier request that you send me at first opportunity your photograph. I would be happy to be able to decorate my home with your picture. My dear wife and I greet and kiss you, as well as all brothers and sisters, relations and acquaintances, not to forget Mrs. Goetzenberger, at whose home you are probably still living.

                    Your loving son, Hannes
                    —— H ——

Washington County 24 August 1851
Dear good Mother!

It is now certain that Ganter will leave here in January for Oregon or somewhere else. In any case I must pay him the 300 dollars that I borrowed from him. I therefore ask you to write me what your situation is, so that, if you cannot loan me the money, I can make other arrangements.
You, dear Mother, have sent me the photograph I requested. A thousand thanks. It will occupy the best place in the best room as long as I live. Unluckily, I must wait till later in the year before I receive the package, which Julius or Franz Wilhelmi will bring to me. Julius is coming here to inspect the country and possibly settle here. My wife was sick 3 weeks and for lack of other help I had to do the house work and serve as nurse and cook, as well as oversee the work on the mill, which, I assure you, was difficult in the summer's heat.

You will therefore not call me a spendthrift when I tell you that I have hired a Negro girl untilthe work on the mill is finished.Although my wife is well now, she is still weak and has to avoid any heavy work. I once tried to do the washing, for 4 persons, but the result was so bad that I gave it up and have never tried laundry work again.

All neighbors within a radius of 15 miles will work on the mill with no charge, several 2 days, others 10 days. Some send their Negroes if they themselves cannot come; others send wagons for my disposition but I have to board and room these people, which makes a lot of work. From the above you can see how important this mill is to this community and I consider myself lucky to be the owner.

The greatest difficulty and the greatest expense is to bring the water to the mill wheel, because the mill race is partly stone masonry and partly (3500 feet) of boards. The soil is porous and stony, and it is in this work that the neighbors will help me.

Yes, dear Mother, I wish you could be eye-witness to our life, not for 3 hours or 3 days, but for week, months, years. I wish this were possible. But your but your quiet withdrawn character, good for this lonesome forest life, would be offset by the fact that you would be deprived of many accommodations to which you have become accustomed and whose loss you would feel keenly. We young people have forgotten the uppity city life. At daybreak in the morning we go to work until sunset in the evening. Food is simple: bacon, milk, eggs, potatoes, cabbage, corn or wheat bread, and now and then honey, then coffee and tea. With occasional changes of menu. Other meat is rare. Chickens are not yet in abundance, and we are not yet in a position to have vegetables regularly.

The house in which we are now living is small, about 15 by 16 feet the inner room, built of logs, with a small porch of which half is boarded up for use as a kitchen, the other half open and can be used as a dining room. The large room itself is crowded with trunks and boxes on which are piled the most necessary articles of clothing and linens. All other things are still in the boxes. On the Walls are _Lwalls_ hanging bags of sugar, coffee, etc., tools, a book case, saddle, etc., etc. In other words there isn't a bit of empty or unused space.

Don't worry about a place for your picture. As soon as the mill is finished, I will have to build a house of three rooms. I'll have to put it in a different location because the place where our house stands is not a healthy location. It is in a low place and surrounded on three sides by the creek and all around the house are tall trees that do not let the breezes through, while the blazing sun heats the cabin. The place where I intend to build the new house is open but against a bluff, is near the mill, and especially it is free of the unhealthy fog that rises each morning and evening from the stream and from the adjoining forest where there are large masses of fallen trees that are rotting and producing harmful and unhealthy gases.

But life here is much different from life in Europe. When one seeks fun or amusement in Europe, he visits the tavern, coffee house, theatre, etc., and thinks he has spent a long tiresome day, if he hasn't drunk a certain quantity of beer or wine and played cards at night.

Here one works lustily all day and when evening comes, I chat with the little woman after supper, while I smoke my pipe, recall things of the past and plan for the future, breathe the clean fresh air, and then go to bed happy and content. But many folks think how unlucky and tiresome our life must be, but I'll bet few of them live as happy a life as we do. Certainly my bacon and cornbread taste better than thousands of their finest dishes. Also, dear Mother, don't worry about your son existing on raw foods and living in a poor cabin. Everything tastes fine and I sleep soundly and feel happy with my little wife. All kind greetings from your loving son

Hannes

—— H ——

Washington County, 16 November 1851

Dear Brother! (to Wilhelm in Lyon)

You offer to loan me money, to be withdrawn from your own business where it will bring you greater interest than I can offer you. Your brotherly heart does not know selfishness and I thank you for your offer. But I think I can get by all right. I thank you for all your advice.

In your letter of 30 September you ask for more details about my life and doings. I will write you everything, although there is little that is pleasing. The mill is not yet in operation and other structures are not as far advanced as I hoped last spring. The reasons are small accidents and the serious illness of my wife. She caught a fever on 4 August, just at the time when I had persons to work, good weather and low water in the creek. I could get no one to nurse her and do the housework and had to do these things myself for four weeks, until I finally hired a Negro girl. She was young, dirty, wasteful and had all the other faults of poorly trained Negroes. However, I was able to oversee and help with the work outside and was glad to have her.

I hired more workmen and everything went la-la until one day Ganter sent a load of wheat to Freyschlag's mill and wanted him to buy other food supplies for me so that I would not be delayed and could keep the workmen busy. But right in the middle of the work, there arrived a messenger from Ganter with a note that two of my horses had run away and I should come immediately to help look for them.

In the meantime, the colored girl had run away and my wife needed my care and the workmen needed supervision. I could not undertake a trip that might require 2 or 3 weeks, because the horses had probably run back to Missouri. So I stayed here. Fourteen days later Ganter came, without the horses, without the wagon, without meal. I at once sent another man after the horses, because I needed the horses in my work. Then the Negress was brought back. So I tried, with my only horse, to get meal and meat, etc., in order not to be delayed in the building. But even this solution did not work, because one morning I found my last and only horse dead in the field. This was really tragic, because she was a fine mare and I expected a fine colt from her.

I now had to get my wagon and flour through rented horses. My wife had made two good recoveries but each time suffered set-backs. So I blamed the location of the house and rented a neighboring farm where I will live till spring, when I will have a new and better house. In order to get immediate possession, I had to loan the owner my wagon for seven days, otherwise I could not move in till New Year. Since I did not have my horses, I agreed. Here my wife made a good recovery, which left me time to work on the mill, along with Ganter and George (a workman he had brought from Missouri). Then I got my horses back, with a bill for 20 dollars. But the wagon was returned in 4 weeks instead of 7 days. During this time we worked on anything that could be done without a wagon but most of which was not too important. We dug the trenches for the foundation walls. Trying to make up for lost time we worked too hard and all three of us got sick. Ganter and George got the fever, and I also had all the symptoms — headache, pains in my arms and legs, and was much tired. Now I, a sick man, had to nurse three other sick persons. Ganter, who saw that he would not receive too good care here, made his way to Freyschlags. I took George into my own home, cured myself while I collected provisions for the winter for man and beast. The sick ones must have suffered while I was away but there was nothing else to be done.

After that, I was able to care for both, my wife and George, so that they soon got better. I succeeded in hiring a better Negress and could again be outdoors and work on the mill where nothing had been done during the preceding weeks. You will be astonished, dear Brother, over all these vicissitudes that, although they did not dull my courage, did cause me much hardship and delayed completion of the mill.

Now the work is progressing finely. The neighbors have been helping me for a week without cost. They would like to see the mill in operation, too costly and troublesome to haul their wheat a long distance. Therefore I hope the mill will be completed by spring.

You wanted an exact account. This is it. Do not let me convince you that my fate and my stay here has been insufferable, not for a moment. On the contrary, I am glad of the future. Any beginning is difficult.

If you are still in the mind of working out a deal with me, then let me know in your next letter how much you can send over here and the exchange rate, so that I can inquire here what the rate is. Perhaps some of the medicinal herbs that grow in this country can be sold in Europe, for example kalmus, sassaparilla roots, slippery elm back, etc.

There is much high living here, in both the large and small cities, but many of these luxuries lack taste. There is much colored/heavy [not too material "a la grisette". Silks and ribbons are expensive but much worn. Double-barrel shotguns are in demand, but 4 and 6-shot pistols will sell more readily. Mule teams are expensive. The ordinary mule [Schonau that of the size that you know in Heidelberg and/Schonau, costs 150 to 300 dollars; larger animals of 12-14 hands high, if they are good as for draught animals, will often bring from 1000 to 1200 dollars. But these are Maltese who reach this height, as little as I know.

—— H ——

Washington County, 11 January 1852
Dear faithful Mother!

I am using the first free Sunday in this new year to write you and send you New Year's greetings and to thank you for all the love that you have shown me in the old year, and to ask for a continuance of your affection. I do not have to tell you that your likeness is constantly in my mind, and that I am trying to be a worthy son.

If I can advise you, dear Mother, let Karl (his brother) come. I wish I had him here now. I will make him work and I'll put callouses on his tender fingers and if he gets accustomed to the work and it pleases him here, then there is room for him. I have plenty for him to do, for several years, but I want him to be a help to me. I pay high wages to my workmen. An ordinary day laborer receives 1 fl 15 kr per day, or 10 dollars (25 fl) per month plus board.

On New Year's day I hired a Negro family (husband, wife and two children) and had to pay 160 dollars per year. W wagon with man and horses costs 2 dollars per day to rent. So you can see that any building costs enormously. The best thing is that even though the expenditures are great, later the income will come, and I am convinced that I will soon be free of debt. Unfortunately, my little wife has been sick for five months and could not run the household during this time. I could not find a good Negress and had to do most of the nursing myself, several times the kitchen work. This naturally prevented me from working on the mill. I stopped work on the mill several times, due to lack of food for the workers and to the Doctor's bill of 70 dollars. In short, I have had a hard and expensive year.

The best thing is that my wife is much better but is still weak. I myself am, thank God, healthy and in good spirits. The package containing your picture, is still with my father-in-law. I have not yet found a way to get it but I hope to soon.

I embrace you in my thoughts,

Your devoted son, Hannes

—— H ——

30 March 1852
Dear dear Mother!

This is a sign of life from an unimportant person, but, thank God, I still am alive and am glad to know that all the other loved ones are in good health. I was sorry to learn that our good Uncle Johann, your brotherly friend and adviser, has died.

The long tiresome fever that plagued me from 4 August until the beginning of January, has left me, I hope forever. I am now in good health, but terribly tired, especially when the weather changes, but that will go away, and I am so glad that I can again manage my own household. Luckily my excellent husband stayed healthy. I cannot tell you enough about his care of me, his self-sacrifice. And if this is the son, what must the Mother be like? He seldom comes into the house without some flowers and then I always think of you and the other dear ones who live so far away.

It would be a big joy to us if Karl could come here, if it would not be your missing him there. Before he leaves, he should consider that all his planning should be directed at the work here and that his only pleasure will be what he accomplishes through the work of his hands. That will be clean and clearer than gold. If, when he comes, he would like to bring a simple and busy lady with him, tell him he will never regret it.

If writing were not so hard for me, I would have long ago written to my brothers and sisters in Germany. I will do so soon. I now again tell a bit about things here. Just now one of my hens, with 11 chicks, is begging at my door and I will feed them. The Negress is plowing. Everything is beautifully green. Please greet all our dear kin, and take care of yourself, dear Mother, and think with love of you

                              - Daughter Nanny
                              --- H ---

Washington County, 4 April 1852
Dear good Mother!

I am satisfied with everything here and am happy. But your oldest son left you and now your second son is nearly ready to do the same. How about the third son - who knows what fate and his restless spirit will lead to? (The youngest brother Eduard who became a pharmacist in Kehl.) This is the end of my lucky and happy thoughts and the beginning of more sober thoughts. Yes, dear Mother, if it were possible to sweeten your declining days by my presence and help, to pay back the debt we owe you for your love and care, I will do it.

From my share of the inheritance from Uncle Johann, please, dear Mother, take for yourself and for Wilhelm, the capital that you loaned me (6000 frs, which I received 10 January), plus interest and costs, and send the rest to me. I do not need any money for building the mill, but if I had the money in hand I could buy wheat and corn much more than the miller can pay us. I can thus make the mill pay out much more easily.

The nearest mill, 8 miles from here, whose location is better than mine and whose water power is not as regular as mine, is for sale at 10,000 dollars and this is the mortgage figure. So, you see, Dear Mother, that I operate under a good loan system. My wife and I are well and think of you often, dear Mother. If nothing prevents, we will get the mill in operation, unless there is a reported American civil was or an American invasion of Europe, of which I have read.

In the hope that these lines will find all of you in good health,
                              I remain your deeply loving son, Hannes
                              --- H ---

Washington County, 25 July 1852
Dear Mother!

Both of the new immigrants have arrived here, after some difficulties and for some time will stay with me and help me to bring the mill in operation. The mill is not yet finished because some things had to be replaced. The axle of the water wheel was rotted inside, which we did not discover until we tried to run it. The wheel itself was not good enough to justify a new axle. So I decided to have it made stronger and permanent. At present I think we can grind in 4 to 6 weeks and there is no doubt but that the mill will soon pay for itself.

We will soon have an entirely German settlement here. George Hackinjos, the laborer that I brought along from Missouri, has bought a place in the neighborhood and will return to Missouri in a few days to get a wife. Also, a Swiss by name of John Ochsner has settled here. Fischer likes it so well that he plans to stay here and will advise several

42

others to stay, since the climate and soil are much better here than in Missouri where the wine industry is already profitable. They figure a gallon from every vine and sell the gallon for 2 dollars.

There is a new law here according to which every head of a family who owns not less than 160 acres of land, becomes the owner if he has lived on the land 5 years, native or immigrant. I could have sold building lots to persons who wanted to start a business near the mill, for example blacksmith shop, store, shoe factory, etc., but I hesitated until the mill was in operation. Then I can get a better price! Much love to all from your

loving son, Hannes

— H —

25 July 1852
Dearly beloved Mother!

With deepest sympathy we read the letters of sister Amelie *Amalie* and poor brother Eduard (Johann's youngest brother) in which they told of your illness and that of the dear brother. Poor Mother, how you must have suffered. How gladly I would like to have helped the sisters in caring for you. We hope and pray that when this letter reaches you, you will long since have recovered. Do let us know, because we always worry when we do not hear from you for any length of time. Take care of yourself and get plenty of rest, now that you are surrounded by your loved ones.

Thank God that we are happy and very busy. We have ten regular workmen, sometimes more, and I always have to beg my dear husband not to work so hard. He naturally wants to get the mill in operation as soon as possible, which is difficult under present circumstances — many things lacking that we had not thought of. They had to cut down the trees and haul them to the sawmill, then bring the boards back here.

Also, my dear husband often has to ride away, to order supplies and make purchases. When he is gone, the workers do not do much work. The Americans here are not a big ashamed to stand around for hours, doing nothing. Then when they hear a wagon coming in the distance, they prick up their ears and wonder who it can be, where he came from, what he was doing there. So they lose several hours work. But the mill will soon be finished and in operation, which will please my dear patient husband very much, after so much expense and such hard work. The cost will be repaid in a short time, all agree, for the prospects are excellent and many persons are jealous of Johann.

On our porch we have two tables placed together, where we take our meals. Our Negress is not a fast worker, so I have to help her a lot to get the food on the table in time. My dear Hannes is always trying to make things easier for his little wife. He surprised me recently with the gift of a pickle slicer which I have used a lot, in canning for the winter. He has made me a grater and other kitchen utensils which I enjoy using because they were made by his own hands.

Life here is a lot like Switzerland. I hear many cowbells in the woods and can tell our own by the tone of the bells. We have three cows that come every morning and evening to be milked. The milk is drunk with the meals and so long as we have many persons to feed, we cannot make much butter and cheese. Later on I will make more butter and cheese because they are German and healthy. The Americans eat a lot of fats, bake pancakes in lard and cover them thick with butter.

Because I was sick in the spring and Hannes was busy building the mill, we could plant only potatoes and necessary things in our garden. There aren't many varieties of vegetables here, so I will try to get other kinds from Missouri. The only flowers in the garden are the many sunflowers which the colored girl planted around the garden. This fall we plan to start a vegetable garden and orchard on our hill, which is not far from our house. Some day it will be beautiful.

Our dear ones in Missouri are well and happy. My parents are getting more accustomed to the entirely different life in the new world. My sister Mina is with them, has four sons, all well. If one is well here then there is nothing lacking, but to be sick here is worse than in Germany. Now I have only enough space left to send greetings and best wishes for your continued well-being. With kisses for you and all the other loved ones

Your loving daughter Nanny Hermann-Wilhelmi

--- H ---

3 September 1852

My dear Mother-in-Law:

Hannes told me this morning that today is your birthday. We wish we could congratulate you in person. I send you today my very best wishes and that you will have many more happy years to enjoy the kinfolks who love you so much. I pray God that you have recovered from your serious illness; also, that dear brother Eduard is better.

We are well and happy. The building of the mill is progressing and we live in happy hopes for the future. We will soon have a city here on our place. Joking aside, several persons -- yesterday there were three -- want to buy property near the mill. They asked Hermann to sell them lots off his land, which he can do at considerable profit. One wan wants to put in a store, another wants to build a blacksmith shop, and so on. As soon as the mill is in operation, the value of our land will increase. People talk of the City of Hermannsburg in fun but also in seriousness. With all kind greetings and kisses for you and the other loved ones,

Your loving, though far-away daughter,
Nanny Hermann

--- H ---

Dear Mother:

I will add my own congratulations on your birthday and wish you many more happy years. My building is progressing rapidly. I have laid out a town on my land and will sell a number of building lots cheaply, to get the town started, after which the price will go up. Two carpenters and one cabinet-maker want several lots on which they plan to build houses for sale. I think my land will soon be populated, after which its value will increase. We are all well and lack nothing except the presence of our old Mami, to whom we would like to show our love and gratitude by giving her our loving care.

Greetings to all
From your loving son Hannes

--- H ---

Washington County, 22 September 1852

Dear Mother:

Yesterday I received your long awaited letter of 8 August. Thank God that you and Eduard are well again. I worried a lot.

I am still living in a rented house near the mill; it is new and quite good. My own house is under construction and I probably will be able to move in by New Year when my lease expires on the rented house. Building goes very slow here and is terrifically expensive. If I had known last year what I know now, I would have asked you to send me, at my expense, three or four workmen. There are many in Germany who do not have the means to make the trip but who could easily earn the cost of the trip over here. It would be advantageous for me to have some good workmen in the neighborhood, especially blacksmiths, wagon-makers, coopers, carpenters, etc., and some good farmers. If you hear of any such, dear Mother, give them my address. I could and will be helpful to them. The location here is as good as anywhere, my place will soon be populated, and tailors and shoemakers can not fail to do a good business.

Ganter went to Oregon last spring. I received a letter from his brother-in-law about four weeks after he left. He had waited for this letter a year, and then had to leave with only 300 dollars, which I owed him and paid him. It is unpardonable that his brother-in-law would deprive a man of a year of his life, for the year was a complete loss for him. Also, he never received the money that Schilling kept for him.

The mill is still not in operation but work goes on and I hope that I can grind the flour for our Christmas baking. I have been offered as much wheat on credit as I can use. Storekeeper Rushel offered me all the wheat that he gets in his big business and I do not have to pay for the wheat until the flour is sold. Several farmers in the vicinity have offered me their entire harvest of from 200 to 500 bushels on credit. But I could do better if I bought for cash.

If Karl wants to come, he should lose no time. Property in the neighborhood of the mill is going up in price. If I had the money now, I would buy for him a farm that adjoins mine which is for sale at 350 dollars. The place on which I am living at present can be bought for 450 dollars -- rich soil, a good house, etc. The owner got into trouble and had to leave. If Karl comes, he should be careful with his money and should always act like a poor man. There are fellows in Havre who make the trip overseas as ordinary passengers, just to find out whom they can "clip", then inform their accomplices in New Orleans and carry out their plans.

Your loving son, Hannes
--- H ---

22 September 1852
My dear Mother!
How glad we are to learn that you, dear Mother, and all the others are in good health. But in Missouri it was otherwise. My dear mother was taken sick on 11 July. She showed apparent improvement on 4 August but the very next day became much worse. She knew she was dying.

45

She became unconscious and fell into a coma that lasted 48 hours. She died unconscious and without suffering.

I can hardly believe that I will never be able to speak to my dear Mother again. My sorrow is great. It is possible that my dear father and poor Lina (Nanny's sister) may visit us but I doubt it, for the journey would be difficult for my father. My mother was already dead when I wrote her a letter telling her a secret that I would tell only to her and to you. But I am in good health and my husband is well and happy about the coming event.

Our congratulations to Karl; we are so glad for him and his intended. Their start here will be much easier than ours because we now know the conditions here and will gladly help them all we can. The two young people from Heidelberg arrived here safely. The smaller one is most helpful because of his diligence and willingness to work. On the other hand, Fischer has been sick with fever ever since he arrived. Even poor George is sick with fever. I think he overtaxed himself at his work. Anyway, he bought a fine horse, intending to leave in a few days, and now he is sick.

We regret that your photograph and the pictures of the brothers and sisters have not arrived. We hoped to get them through George. I had been looking forward with so much pleasure to seeing you all and now I must wait patiently.

When I think of Missouri, I am filled with sadness. If I could have seen her just one more time. The others are well. My brother Julius has built a good double house.

Here we hope that by NewYear we can get into at least one room inour new house on the hill. That is when we will have to leave the house where we now are. I can recommend this place to a good German family. I would be so glad to have good German neighbors. My Hermann has a different place in mind for Karl. We would so much like to have more good Germans in our neighborhood. They will never regret coming here, because there are so many opportunities and money to be made. We no longer worry about the fever. Anywhere in America a newcomer has to experience some unpleasantness, some more, some less, until he becomes acclimated, then everything is well. This is true in other situations as well. There are some things that one has to get used to and some things that are better forgotten.

Just now my dear Hannes is coming up the hill from the mill. He has on his blue cotton shirt, such as American workmen wear, and pants that came from the Fatherland, and a black felt hat. He will finish our letter to the dear Mother in Germany, while his little wife goes into the kitchen to see if the colored woman has put the beef and cabbage on the fire, for our noonday meal.
N.B. To Karl and his intended I would advise that they bring a good German girl along, until he has an opportunity to buy a good Negress. They will have to have someone to help with the house work. A poorly trained slave is of little value. The good ones are seldom hired out and cannot be easily bought. Also, it would be much more home-like, at least at the beginning when one cannot speak English, to have a white German girl around the house. So, adieu! Many hearty greetings to all relations and a special child-like kiss for you, dear Mother, from

Your true and loving Nanny

ELISE HERMANN NUESSLE
1853 — 1920
who related the childhood memories of Old Hermannsburg, Washington
County, Arkansas.

CHILDHOOD MEMORIES OF A GERMAN-AMERICAN GIRL

as told by Elise Nuessle, nee Hermann

(Editor's note: The article that follows contains the childhood memories of John H. Hermann's daughter Elise, who was born in Washington County, Arkansas, in 1852. She became Mrs. Adolf Nuessle of Mannheim, Germany. She told these memories to her granddaughter, Gertrud Gscheidlen (now Mrs. Alfred Meyer) who recorded them. Our translation is from a typescript in German that was furnished by Prof. and Mrs. W. E. Meyer of State College, Pennsylvania, to whom we are most grateful. — WJL) ⨯ They were edited in the „Badische Heimat"?

—— H ——

On the Farm

Among the many Germans who emigrated in the year of the 1848 revolution was a young engineer from Mannheim, John Henry Hermann, who had been educated in Vienna, Mailand, and Florence and who had received his practical training in Lyon. Traveling with him to America was a preacher named Wilhelm Wilhelmi with the latter's two sons and two daughters. John Henry Hermann associated himself with the two Wilhelmi sons and several other young men in a bachelor housekeeping set-up on a farm in Missouri, which they named Wilhelmi Farm.

They shared the household duties: one was in charge of the kitchen for a week, another brought firewood from the forest, and still another did the washing. The result was so entertaining that they quite forgot the difficulties they had anticipated. One of the men had such a poor sense of direction that he could only find his way out of the forest with difficulty, so they tied a cow-bell around his neck, and when they no longer heard the bell tinkle, one of the comrades would go to seek him, knowing surely that he had lost his way. White and woolen wash were placed in the same washtub of boiling water until all the articles had turned a dirty gray.

So they looked around for feminine housekeepers, who were not hard to find, since the sisters, Nanny and Lina Wilhelmi, lived nearby. John Henry married Nanny and looked around for a new home.

Wedding Journey to Arkansas

In a beautiful hilly area, on the border of Arkansas and the Indian Territory, surrounded by primeval forests and prairies covered by cane as tall as a man, lay a small valley between two hills. A creek meandered through the meadows which were thickly covered with flowers. All around stood unusual trees. This place was the objective of their journey after the wedding.

The young couple rode in a wagon, driven by a hired hand. They said goodbye to the Wilhelmi parents who promised to follow them soon. It was thought that the trip would take several weeks and so they took plenty of food with them. Each evening they camped. The horses were unhitched, a fire was made on the ground, coffee was brewed and wild meat broiled over the fire. Meat was plentiful and free, for there was no law forbidding the use of the forest and its treasures.

There were also adventures -- peaceful ones.   One night they were
awakened suddenly by the shaking of the wagon. At first they thought
it was an earthquake but discovered that wildhogs were rubbing against
the wagon and threatening to upset it.   On another occasion they en-
countered a terrific storm but it was daylight and the storm soon
passed. In that region there is tropical heat in the summer but no ice
or snow in winter, only a wet season of several weeks.

Hermannsburg

The little caravan finally reached the valley. They first lived in a
small log cabin until the big new house, already being built on top of
the hill, could be finished.   Building naturally proceeds more slowly
than in Europe because materials and workmen can be secured only with
difficulty.   Farmers of the neighborhood helped and could be assured
that they would be repaid in like manner.

In the low place where the log cabin stood, the air was humid and
unhealthy, so that the young wife became very ill with malaria. Other
dangers threatened, especially snakes and poisonous plants.   One day
when the sick Nanny was alone at home, lying helpless on her bed, she
saw a large rattlesnake on the rafter of the cabin. The snake came at
regular intervals to feed a nest of young snakes. John came at the
right time, seized his gun and fired a load of shot into the snake's
speckled body, so that it fell dead from the rafter.

Finally the beautiful new house was finished and they moved in. They
gave the name of Hermannsburg to their property. Much later the Americans named the site Dutch Mills meaning German Mills. Most Americans
called all Germans Dutch. We seldom heard the word "German".

John then built a mill, which was at first driven by water power.
The water had to be brought a considerable distance through a flume of
hollowed-out logs.   Water power was later replaced by steam but the
boiler and other machinery had to be brought from the East.

The work in the open, while tending his crops and while building the
house and the mill, pleased John so much that he wrote to his worrying
mother in Germany: " Now I am a human being. I cannot describe how
happy I am."

Time passed.   John's brother Fritz complained of the hard times in
Germany and thought he could better himself as merchant if he emigrated to America. So John wrote to him, inviting him to come to Hermannsburg where a store was needed.   He advised him that the ocean voyage
would take from six to eight weeks, hence he must supply himself with
coffee, sugar, dried meat, a pillow and a blanket.

Father Hermann, druggist in Mannheim, had meanwhile retired and
lived in Heidelberg, where he died.   The Mother Hermann could hardly
bear to see a second son depart for America. Fritz arrived in Hermannsburg on 28 April, 1853 — I was exactly two days old! The grandmother
in Heidelberg was anxious to know about all of us, so My Uncle Fritz
placed my hand on a sheet of paper and traced the outline of my hand,
so that my grandmother would have proof of her first grandchild.

--- H ---

Grandfather Wilhelm Wilhelmi

When I was about six months old, our dear grandfather Wilhelmi came from Missouri. His wife had died. Because he had been a preacher in Germany (24 years in Stebbach and later in Bauschlott),he baptized me. two years later (1855) my sister Minna was born, then brother Wilhelm (1856) and Julia Amalia (1857).

We grew and prospered. Grandpa was a busy little man. He worked in the garden or fields, just as he pleased. He cultivated the rose bushes and fruit trees and took care of the bee-hives, as if he had never done anything else. His image is still so clear to me. I can see him with his red cheeks and snow-white hair, lost in thought. Wearing his red-trimmed robe, with his long pipe that he lit with tinder and on which he puffed constantly, even when the fire had gone out, he would seat himself at the window, after a hard day's work. We children would gather around him and he would tell us the most beautiful fairy tales. In addition to Red Riding Hood he would tell us the most fantastic stories of his own invention and the bigger our eyes became, the greater his flights of fancy. We liked especially the story of the "Half Chicken" who went traveling and conquered every obstacle -- if he couldn't fly over a creek, he drank it up, and when the barn in which he was camping caught fire, he put out the fire with the water he had drunk from the creek. When we shuddered or screamed in excitement he would tell us to hush and promised to continue his stories. I was the most insistent that he tell us a story, so he nicknamed me "Tell us something." And when I kept clamoring for more stories, he said: "Now, there was once a shepherd who had many sheep and a fine dog. One day they had to cross a pond on a narrow board and the sheep could only cross one at a time. That took a long time and it was to-morrow before they arrived on the other side of the pond. So I cannot tell you the rest of the story today."

Birds and Animals, Flowers and Trees

The plant and animal world were magnificent in their beauty and in their danger. The danger gave them a special attraction for us children. We were not too closely watched and could wander around the farm as we pleased, as long as we were not naughty or disobedient. We did not call for help when we saw a snake but crushed the snake's head with a rock.

In the garden were lovely flowers, from which Grandfather's bees gathered honey and carried it to the hives. And what a treat when the comb filled with honey painted our faces with luscious sweetness!

The juice of the cane looked a lot like honey and when it came from the press we imagined it would taste just as good as honey. I once filled myself with its sweetness, after having been warned, and after that one experience I never again ate cane juice.

We also had sweet potatoes, long and reddish. They tasted like almonds, both when raw and when cooked. Alongside the melons, squash, and sweet potatoes, there grew Spanish peppers, a scarlet fruit about 6 to 8 inches in length.

The flowers in the garden were unusually fragrant. From the roses to the most ordinary flowers they would be swarmed with bees and the loveliest of birds, the humming bird, who would sink their long bills into the bloom while their wings vibrated at such speed that we could hardly see the color of the bird.

Another interesting bird was the whippoorwill, the American nightingale, whose melodious call "Whip-poor-will" sounded in early evening. The name comes from the days of slavery and translated means "Peitsch den armen Will!" — "Whip poor Will."

There is no twilight, even as there is no Spring. The star-lit heavens defy description. Lightning bugs also illuminate the night.

A row of peach trees ran along the edge of the garden. When the big juicy fruit did not drop fast enough, we children would climb up into the trees and make a meal - breakfast, dinner or supper - of peaches.

When we wanted eggs, we hunted in the bushes, for the chickens there were not cooped up or fed. They find plenty of feed outside and have only a little roof in the yard for refuge at night and from rain and thunderstorms.

The cows also were driven out in the pasture and returned each evening by themselves to the barn. We drank the milk raw, fresh from the cow. My sister Minna, the boldest of all of us children, even dared to lie under the cow and suck the milk. We also had goats. Animals that were to be slaughtered were shot.

An edible animal is the turtle, which makes very tasty soup. The turtle's shell is as large as a dough-pan. The shells were used as work baskets.

An especially beautiful tree is the hickory, of which there were a great number on our farm. The wood is pliable and we liked to climb up into the hickory trees. Once Minna climbed into the very top of a hickory tree and swung back and forth so that it looked as if a storm were raging in the branches. In the midst of her swinging, our Mother appeared on the scene. Although frightened, she remained quiet so as not to frighten the child, and ordered her to climb down. Minna came down, not suspecting anything, but as soon as she felt solid ground beneath her feet she also felt the solid hand of her Mother on her tree-happy bottom ("baumlustigen Sitzteil")! We were seldom spanked and then only by our Mother or Grandfather — usually for damaging young fruit trees or something like that.

Incidentally, it may be told that American women of the West — the genuine Yankeedoodles — have an "elegant" custom. They take the tender shoots of the hickory, cut them into the length of a cigaret, and chew one end into a brush-like point. Charcoal and salt are ground together and carried in a small box. The chewed wood is then dipped in the black powder, rubbed on the teeth and cached in the cheek. Now and then they bite off the end, chew it again, spit, and continue. In the meantime they can put on an impressive appearance.

There were no grapes, except a variety that grows wild, climbs up on oak trees, and has small blue-black berries in big bunches. Their taste is sour-sweet.

Mother Nanny

Household management on a farm is naturally not comparable with the so-called "managed" European system; and those who managed households in Hermannsburg considered their important duties from an idealistic standpoint. Her most precious possession was her children, and she worked day and night not only for our physical needs but she taught us German, reading and writing, taught us to pray and told us the Bible stories. She often said that her favorite Bible passage was the Sermon on the Mount. In her German hymn-book she had marked her favorite songs. And on the white pages of that book she entered the birthdays of her children.

Mother did not have to work in the garden. But it was necessary for her to make the sausage at slaughtering time, and she was most successful in producing a large quantity of tasty sausage.

She also made our candles. She would take several tin tubes about the thickness of a candle, put in a cotton wick, pour in the melted fat, and when it had cooled, we had a light. There was no other means of illumination. But the nights were not long and people had time for their day's work.

In the meantime our Uncle Fritz had opened a store in the middle of our valley. From time to time he would travel to St. Louis, Missouri, and purchase his wares. I always/ordered candy but seldom saw any. *I thought that would mean*
On the opposite side of the valley, across the creek, on a neighboring hill, Uncle Fritz had built his home. His wife was Aunt Lina, sister of my Mother. She also had children, three boys, Henry, Edward and Louis, whom we put up with or feuded with, depending on how we felt. Also in the neighborhood was the home of my Mother's brother, Uncle Julius, and soon came her sister, Aunt Minna, with her husband, the Reverend Eberld, and three sons, from Germany. The Eberles eventually had eight children.

One day an unusually large box was delivered at our house. When the boards were removed, a metal case made its appearance. The space in between was filled with excelsior, straw and paper, in which were packed the most beautiful dolls and tin doll furniture — the most beautiful toys. We had never seen anything like it. But the most important thing of all soon stood before our astonished eyes — a piano, from Heidelberg, from Grandmother Hermann! Now our mother gave us a
lessons by her piano/recital. We were deliriously happy. She was an excellent teacher. While she played we learned to knit and crochet, seated beside her *and the*. When I grew tired, Mother would say "Lie down and sleep a while." And when I had rested for about an hour, the knitting came much easier. So it was with piano lessons also; I learned very easily. From Mother's later letters I learned that it was always her wish that I might con- *there was no doubt I would do so.* tinue with my music, which at that time did not seem possible. But I *thus* did, much later, reach the concert stage.

At night, after we had been tucked in bed, our Mother would play and sing. And when she thought us asleep, I would raise my head from the pillow and call out "More, more!"

Free Hours

When our mother was sewing clothes on her Wheeler & Wilson sewing machine, we children with our cousins would run to the creek for swimming. In the willow stumps along the shore lay a tangled mass of water snakes, sunning themselves. Now and then one would stretch up a head to examine the vicinity. We were not afraid of them, for this species is not poisonous. Stark naked we ran into the watter and suddenly the snakes also dived in with a loud splashing. Suster Julie cried out, "A snake, a snake!" But when we examined her, we found a bloodsucker (leech) on her leg, which we soon rendered harmless.

[margin handwritten note: L water]

We would hunt large, long, smooth stones on the banks of the creek, for which we made doll dresses. What a wonderful world of fantasy they evoked!

If the boys were naughty, I, as the oldest, would scold them. They would then tease me by calling me "the baptized", for I was the only one who had been baptized. At that time there was no church in the neighborhood, but later my brothers and sisters were also baptized.

My most precious possession was a pony, but I was seldom permitted to ride it, only when we made family excursions, as for example to the Freyschlag farm. There lived a family with many children, in a beautiful house with a large veranda.

Indians

The Indians in that area were mostly Cherokee. We children seldom saw them. They transacted their business with our Father and Uncle. Father got along very well with them, since he had shown them many kindnesses by furnishing them with flour and other foodstuffs. They spoke English with him, something they ordinarily did not like to do. The Indians made their living by hunting and each year would go to the fur market in St.Louis where they would sell the pelts of beavers and other animals.

My Father was the doer of good deeds in that entire region. He was known far and wide as "Doktor Alles" (Doctor of Everything). If someone was sick, he was summoned. If the cow did not give milk or if the clock stopped, Dr. Everything could help. Whenever he found a sick or helpless man on the road, he would take him home, give him nourishment and medicine and sometimes nurse him for weeks. And it occasionally happened that the persons whom he helped would steal from him. But "giving alms never made anyone poor", and although Father was not as well off in this world's goods as Uncle Fritz, he had other rewards.

One time our Uncle Julius hired an Indian as a wood-cutter. At mealtime Uncle took the man with him to family dinner, because he enjoyed seeing the Indian's astonishment at European things in the house. Uncle's wife, Aunt Luise (nee Langfried from Heidelberg), had on this particular day prepared noodles.The Indian ate and ate until it seemed he would burst. Finally he asked what these things really were. Just for fun, Uncle told him "Those are shredded pig's intestines." The Indian pushed his plate away and could not be induced to eat anything else -- he felt bad.

[margin handwritten note: L Langfried]

54

Negroes

Negroes brought over from Africa were used for heavy work out-of-doors because they could stand the heat better than the whites. These Negroes were bought and sold, their families torn apart, and they were driven with a whip to work in the cotton and cane-sugar fields. We had no such plantations in our area, and my Father fought with word and deed for the abolition of slavery.

We once took a Negro child that had become separated from its parents when they were sold to a distant place. We had a lot of fun with the "Niggerle" because of his ~~dumbness~~ *L stupidity*. He did not even know that people wore under-clothing. He wore only a ~~shirt~~ *L little dress*. When we put him in bed, he would not lie still but wrapped himself in the coverlet and cowered in a corner of the room. So he had to sleep in the kitchen. At night he would cry a lot, come to the door, knock and beg to be let in — he was afraid. One day we asked him where his shirt was. He said he had thrown it out in the rain to wash it.

School

How often we heard about schools and how we longed for schools that were not available in Arkansas. Then it occurred to an elderly American to gather all the children in the neighborhood in a log cabin and teach them what little he knew. We begged our parents to let us attend this school and did not stop begging until they gave their consent. The man did not speak a word of German, so we had to order English reading books. The cabin was deep in the wilderness, so we had to ride there each day. An old and tame horse was found and that banished all obstacles. My cousin Otto Wilhelmi, my sister Minna and I, the three comrades under Mother's instruction, were placed on the horse, and we were on our way. A tin bucket of sour-milk, bread and cold meat in our pockets — that was our noon meal.

This place in the woods was very beautiful. A number of eager boys and girls, aged 6 to 12 and older, found themselves in one room. The boys sat on one side, the girls on the other. Names were unimportant. We soon got acquainted with the stock-Americans. We memorized, with deep sincerity the simple verses in the reader. If we could not work the problems, or if we were naughty, the teacher never punished by spanking. He made the guilty girl sit with the boys and vice versa. We would cover our face for shame.

At noon we had recess, in which we could play outdoors until the teacher pounded three times on the door, the signal for resumption of our instruction. Our noon meal we ate beside a spring, which furnished us our drinking water. The spring was shaded from the heat by a huge walnut tree whose scented leaves hung down to us. We made cup-shaped drinking vessels out of the leaves. The teacher ate under another tree some distance away. He ate eagerly and his meal was probably washed down with whisky.

Sickness and Death

When we were sick, especially with fever, we were always treated with a cold water cure. It was a sore trial to be wrapped in a wet cloth. One day this happened to me but I bit my teeth together and suffered bravely. As soon as I was allowed to get up again, I hastened into my garden, a little plot that I was allowed to cultivate myself. Just look! In those few days the beans had come up -- the little green shoots were just out of the earth. The peas and lettuce had come up, and on the smooth earth where nothing had yet been planted, I saw to my great delight tracks like those of little angels' feet. In my happiness I wrote in my note-book: "Dear Mama, now I know why God has let my garden grow so beautifully -- because I was so brave when I was wrapped in the wet cloth."

At that time, when I was eight years old, I suffered an attack of the Egyptian eye disease and for three weeks I was totally blind. My Father did not try his medical tricks on me; lukewarm packs that were constantly changed, cleaned and healed my eyes.

Our Father pulled our first teeth. When he said "Let me see if it is loose", we knew enough. With a skillful grasp he pulled the loose tooth. He never used force but rather tried to convince us of the necessity of his measures.

One day I saw Aunt Luise standing in tall grass that almost hid her. A goat came running at her and butted her with his horns, so that she disappeared. I do not remember if this had anything to do with her death, but that night the dog bayed so mournfully and on the following day our poor Aunt died. It was the first death in the family. She was buried in the forest.

The year 1860 arrived and with it the birth of the youngest brother, Oscar. But before that, Grandfather had said to our Mother: "Tomorrow afternoon at half past 3 o'clock, give the children each a piece of my biscuit and a swallow of my Malaga." This was unusual, that we dared taste Grandfather's sacred wine, for on previous occasions when he had let us "try" it, this consisted of pressing the palm of the hand against the open bottle which we turned upside down, and then licking the few drops of wine from our hand. On the following morning, he did not make his usual appearance and when we went to look for him, he was lying on the floor. A stroke had hit him and at half past 3 o'clock that afternoon he was dead. Our grief can be imagined. When our Mother said her last farewell to him, she bent over the casket and kissed him on his brow. He found his last resting place in the forest.

At about the same time, our dear Mother became seriously ill, and we had to take Baby Oscar to Aunt Lina to care for. And when Mother finally was able to get up and get around on crutches, a new terror struck, with the report "War has come!"

War

The Americans of the North had finally decided to force the South to free the slaves. Our German colony, with my Father at the head, stood at the side of the Northerners (Union) although surrounded by enemies. Because our enemies threatened my Father's life, President Lincoln offered to protect us Germans and permitted my Father and my Uncle to join the Northern army where they were useful in the Sanitary Commission.

We children, greatly downcast, rode to school. The pupils were all
there, only the teacher was missing. When a pair of curious boys went
out to see if the teacher was coming, they returned suddenly, crying
"He is coming!" And he appeared, walking shakily as if he had imbibed
a bit too much on hearing the war news. He sang out, "Children, children, war is coming. Hurry that you get away!" We saddled our Rosinante
and from that moment school was a past experience for us.

When my Father and his brother secured a leave and wanted to see if
we were still alive, they hid in a cave in our neighborhood. At night
they would approach the house cautiously and knock on the door. Homesickness and fear for him pressed us more than the terror we suffered
when Southerners or bushwhackers (plunderers) came and took the little
we had left. But our greatest fear was when they threatened to hang
our Father.

One afternoon a band arrived and demanded a saddle. Although we told
them that we did not have a saddle, they threatened us with a loaded
revolver and said: "Woe to you if we find one." They took as much
clothing as they could carry, but when one took Grandpa's long tobacco
pipe, my Mother tore it away from him with the words: "You leave that
here!" He became bolder and when he left he said: "Madam, I shall come
back." From that time on, our Mother carried a deer knife under her
dress and said: "Truly, I knew how to use it."

Once when a troop of Southern soldiers galloped by and saw the then
5-year-old Wilhelm on the road, one of them called: "Look here, the
little Union man! Catch him!" They caught him and were amused when he
fought and screamed, lifted him on a horse, and when they finally let
him go, they threatened to hang his father.

Strangers told us that our Father had been wounded. They said that
they had seen the blood stream from his head.Later it developed that it
wasn't blood they had seen but a red cloth that he had bound around
his head because of an infection of his eyes. Once he was in mortal
danger when a wounded soldier whom he was trying to help, continually
cried: "Doctor, the world is coming to an end", and in his irrational
fever clamped his hands on Father's throat. Just in the nick of time
he was freed from the crazy man's grasp.

At intervals there was peace and quiet and Aunt Lina, who, with her
three boys lived with us, could return to her own home. But she had to
promise our Mother that she would make a sign if danger threatened.
Aunt Lina had a large sea-shell which gave an echoing sound. She was
to blow this if there was danger.

Shortly after, when Mother had barely laid down to sleep, a dozen
men forced their way into the house. She quickly put on her clothes.
One man, wearing a big drooping hat, sat down opposite her while the
others searched the house for gold. They did not want paper money.
They pulled the children out of their beds; slit open the mattresses;
in short, they turned the whole house upside down. Suddenly the ugly
man who was guarding my Mother, said to her in perfect German: "Madam,
do not move. At the slightest sound I shall press the trigger; my revolver is loaded. But if you remain quiet, I can help you." This he
said in perfect German, and continued: "I am the son of good parents,
but since the war started I have been a devil. But I shall protect the
Germans, for I myself am a German." At his urging, the band soon left.

57

When Aunt Lina heard them come, she had gone up on the porch and had
blown the conch-shell. We heard the long-drawn-out call for help and
knew that she was in danger, but we could not help her for the storm
had torn away the bridge over the creek. Aunt Lina took her St. Bernard
dog into the room with her, and when the gang came, the dog arose with
his clinking chain at the window. The robbers saw something glistening
in the moonlight, thought it might be soldiers, and left.

Finally they broke into Uncle's store and threw all the goods that
they did not want into the street, among them some white and black
porcelain dolls. They forced their way into the mill but found only a
sack of bran, used for cattle feed. But they were so starved that they
ate it, in spite of the worms that it contained.

In our neighborhood there were several decisive battles. We saw the
fleeing Indians on their horses galloping past. Their women had the
children bound on their backs.

Then came the seizure of our home for officers' quarters — 18 officers at one time. All around us on the heights were campfires, so that
it looked as if the whole forest was afire.

Flight

So the year 1862 approached its end. It was about the middle of December when my Father whispered to my Mother that we would have to flee
in order to save our lives. He told her to pack what was needed. So we
began to shoot the chickens and salt them for keeping. Bread was baked
to last for several weeks. And then one day a large wagon drove up to
the house, covered with canvas. The beds were piled in the wagon and
we children on top of them, with a strange woman in charge of us. It
was the first time that we had been separated from our Mother, which
was a great sacrifice on her part. But there was no other way out. Our
Father was helpless with severe back pains and the baby Oscar had the
measles, so our Mother had to ride with them in another wagon. The
journey began. At night and in fog, like fleeing thieves, we left our
fine estate, which shortly afterwards went up in flames. Only the
piano was saved and taken to Uncle Eberle for safe-keeping.

Just as ten years before the young couple had arrived in Arkansas in
one wagon, so they now left this little spot of earth that had been
their paradise. Through empty fields where far and wide not a house
was to be seen, through prairies of tall grass, through forests with
trackless brush, we traveled on. On Christmas Eve we arrived in a field
where shortly before a battle had taken place. Homesickness drove me
to my Mother. With a simple "Everything has to have an end", she con-
soled me. A campfire was lit and Mama kneaded a dough of water and meal
and baked flat cakes. Those were our Christmas goodies. That night we
slept in the ruins of a burned house whose owner had fled. Before we
went to bed our Father took us outside, pointed at the star-lit heavens, and said, almost weeping: "Those are your Christmas lights."

In Washington, Missouri

After four weeks we arrived in the lovely little town of Washington,
where we were greeted by Uncle Franz, my Mother's brother, and his
wife, our Aunt Alwine. Uncle Franz was an officer in the Northern army
and so we had excellent protection. Shortly after our arrival we all

58

became ill as a result of the trip. Our Mother nursed us through the measles. Near the end of April she herself became ill and had to go to bed. She wanted our Father to be her doctor but he thought the responsibility too great and also there were graduate physicians in that community. So two doctors were called in but she became weaker and weaker.On the eighth day she asked me to stay at her side because she was feeling so bad. I did not think it was so serious and in my childish carefree way I went into the garden. That night -- I slept in the adjoining room -- I heard her heavy breathing. I remembered that my Mother had taught me to pray, so I began the Lord's Prayer. When I reached "Thy will be done", I could not continue.-- I thought how can I be willing for my Mother to die? I fell asleep. When I awoke I knew that we were to lose more than gold and property. Our Mother,breathing heavily and deathly pale, said to Father: "Give me my diary -- and you write the ending." She meant the diary in the form of letters to her sisters living in Germany. The diary is still in existence. Those were her last words. The calendar showed 30 April, 1863.

My Father took each of us in his arms, wept in his agony, and said: "You no longer have a Mother." We were all there when she was laid to rest in a real cemetery.

Then our Aunt Lina took us to her home, adding us to her three children. There was almost no room in the house, so she sent us to school in the daytime. We were glad to go to school. A German teacher took us under his command. The boys here were lazier and naughtier than in Arkansas. During recess they jumped out of the windows and carried on all sorts of mischief. Punishment was the same as in Arkansas. Except for that, I have no memories, either of the school or of life in that community. Everything was without savor.

At this sorrowful time there arrived a letter from Aunt Amalie, the childless sister of my Father in Mannheim. This letter was to change everything. She had received the letter with the news of Mother's death and wrote immediately that my Father should bring his five motherless children to her -- she would be their mother.

Trip on the Steamship "Harmonia"

So we got ready for the trip to Europe. We had a railroad trip of several days to survive before we reached the ocean. My Father made me responsible for my younger brothers and sisters and if he had to leave us for even a minute he would put me in the middle of the group and have me hold on to each one's clothing. We were not frightened by the locomotive, although it was an unknown monster to us, and we were very happy to climb aboard the steamship in New York harbor.

Naturally we refugees attracted much interest, because everyone on the ship soon knew of the war-time tragedy that had befallen us. The cabin in which we slept had four beds, two below and two above. On one side of the room, my Father and Wilhelm slept in the upper bunk, and Oscar and Julchen below. On the other side, at the round porthole that looked out on the sea, I slept, with Minna in the lower bed.

The arrangement pleased us so much that Minna and I, especially I, became quite bold. One evening I decided to frighten her, so I brushed my hair down over my face and hung my head down above her bed, so that my face appeared to her upside-down. The next night she got revenge by pushing me up with the whole bed.

The evenings were lovely but I had to watch Oscar. In order to get up on deck, I would draw the curtains on his bed and say, "Now go to sleep." But he wasn't so easy to satisfy and cried: "Eli, Eli, stay with me." So I tried a trick: "Yes, I'll stay; take the corner of my apron and hold on tight." He was soon asleep, so I took off my apron, and away I went. He held the corner of the apron fast in his little hands while I could see the big beautiful ocean at night.

In Mannheim

We were welcomed in Mannheim with real joy and after the first excitement had subsided, we saw ourselves in changed circumstances and made friends with our new foster-parents.

The next thing that my poor Father did was to complete his medical education. It had always been his ambition to be a doctor, so he enrolled in the University of Heidelberg and studied there two years. Students called their 38-year-old fellow-student "Uncle" and this nickname stayed with him for many years. He knew that he would not be allowed to practice medicine in Germany, so he decided to return to America, to St.Louis, Missouri.

Meanwhile we children also entered school, this time in the Evangelical public school. Everyone had heard that the "little Americans" would enter the school and when we really showed up, there was a regular riot. All wanted to be with us during recess. They finally got used to us and to the fact that we weren't coal-black as they had thought.

The teacher had an instrument that I had not seen before -- a switch which on this particular day he used on every member of the class because one pupil had been noisy. The switching did not hurt me but I was angry over what I felt was unfair treatment.

After a half year I transferred to the girls' school in the castle, where, because of my eleven years, I was immediately put into the fourth grade. I could read and write German better than the others, even though they had been in school three years.

The two years which my Father had allotted for his studies had now passed and it was necessary for him to think of his departure. He had made his reservation on a certain ship when he had a most unusual experience. He had a vivid dream that his dead wife said to him: "Don't be so hasty. He is a fool who sails in a storm." Unbelievable as it may sound, the warning was so clear and urgent that he decided to take a later ship. He had no need to regret his decision -- the first ship went down on the journey.

The parting was difficult. I was then twelve years old but my Father carried me in his arms like the other children, walked up and down the room and wept quietly. It was his parting from a child that he never again saw as a child.

-- WCHS --

60

WAR

(Reprinted from "Flashback", Volume IX Number 4, Washington County Historical Society, Fayetteville, Arkansas.)

The Hermann brothers of Washington County, Arkansas, had married the Wilhelmi sisters, Lina and Nani, of Franklin County, Missouri. Lina was the wife of Karl Hermann; they had three children, all born in Washington County. Nani was the wife of Johann Herman; they had five children, all born in Washington County.

The brother of these sisters, Franz Wilhelmi, was Captain of Co.C, 17th Missouri Volunteers USA. This put the Hermanns in a dangerous position in Washington County and it was necessary for Karl and Johann Hermann and other men of the settlement to hide out in the woods at night, leaving their families unprotected.

The wives of these men kept a diary, which was published (in German) after the war. We have translated and are publishing the diary entries for November and December 1862. They give a graphic picture of what war was like for women and children.

— H —

From the Diary of Lina (Mrs. Karl) Hermann

Nov. 12, 1862 - We live in constant fear and danger. It is said that all men must join the Southern army. A negro stole horses, saddles and took my Melinda with him. We have been considered sympathizers for the South so far but if the Northern troops come we will openly declare ourselves. Today starving secessionists were in our mill and acted as if it were their property.

Nov. 13 - The Pin Indians are stealing everywhere.

Nov. 14 - Today we saw Southern troops for the first time. We heard shooting and about 200 Confederates came galloping through the village pursued by Northern troops. I hid the children in the cellar.

Nov. 15 - When I awoke at 4 o'clock this morning, I thought everything was on fire. I ran to the window and saw everywhere camp fires soldiers and horses, but did not know if they were Southerners or Northerners. It turned out they were part of Hindman's Confederate army. I have been ordered to cook for the soldiers. I have tied a bandage over one eye and tell them I am not well and will cook only for the sick and wounded. I am tired of cooking for secessionists. Nani cooks for them and out of gratitude four soldiers stole everything they could lay hands on, from her.

Nov. 16 - The troops have gone north and we fear for the safety of our men folks. We dare not undress to sleep and even the children sleep with their clothes on.

Nov. 17 - This uncertainty is terrible. The women are despairing.

Nov. 18 - Several men broke into our store and stole much. I ran through the rain to Schmitt who came over and nailed up the house.

Nov. 20 - As I stood at the window two men rode up. One was Fritz, and oh, what joy! All the women of the neighborhood came over. At midnight Julius came and said they would have to leave immediately. Fritz didn't want to leave us alone again, but I knew his danger and insisted that he go.

Nov. 23 - Last night I took the children over to Nani's and stayed with her. Tonight she is with me. A group of Northern soldiers stopped and I gave them a letter to my husband. Three hours later General Marmaduke came with several thousand men. I let the rebels look into my empty flour bin and told them J had been cooking and baking for their men all week and would have to keep my little remaining food for my children. So they didn't get my hidden meal, but did take pigs and chickens. At night I took faithful Nero in the room with us.

(Mina's)

Nov. 25 - Today I heard that Southern troops were at Mina's house so I went over and found the house full of soldiers. They wanted all the food she had, but she told them that all pigs, hay and corn had already been taken. Marmaduke promised to pay her, but all she got from his secretary was $10 in Confederate money. It is now generally known that our men folks are in the Northern camp and we may as well be prepared to have all our possessions taken by the Southern troops. Mina and I agreed to stay 14 days longer and then to flee with what little food we have left. Nani is opposed to the idea because it is too cold for the children. And Fritz might return.

Dec. 8 - My man has returned with 28 Northerners. Maria is helping me prepare food for them. Fritz is packing up goods to take to the Northern camp to sell. At night they all left. I feared Fritz would enter the Northern army as a soldier but he promised to wait a while.

Dec. 9 - Nani is with me. All day long we heard cannonading. Who will be victorious? This constant thundering of the cannon! If the Southern troops should win, it would go hard with us.

Dec. 14 - It is said the Southern troops were victorious. I don't believe it. Last night three soldiers dressed in blue demanded admittance. I had the dog beside me, so let them in. They demanded money and when I told them there was none, they searched the entire house and took what they wanted. I offered them Confederate money but they refused that. One of them threatened me with his gun and I was glad Fritz wasn't there. They took coffee, flour, clothing, handkerchiefs, and keepsakes that we had brought from Germany. They remained in the house two hours and left.

Dec. 15 - Every day they come, sometimes to Nani and sometimes to my house. I have baked bread for three days and before I can give it to the children, it is taken away from me. The children are crying. Our desperation is great.

Dec. 18 - Fritz came today with a military escort of 100 men. He says we will leave tomorrow. How gladly I will leave here. Only the parting from Mina will hurt, that and the fact that I will have to leave my beautiful piano here, on which my Heinrich plays so well.
                                                        — Lina

From the Diary of Nanni (Mrs. Johann Hermann)

Nov. 14, 1862 - Yesterday our mill ran all day grinding meal for the starved Southern soldiers. Toward noon we heard shooting. We were afraid there would be a battle in our village. However, the Southern soldiers fled and the Pin Indians, Northern sympathizers, came. At Eberle's and other neighbors the Indians stole horses. Julius followed the Indians and brought the horses back. Mina was almost shot when three Southerners sought to hide in her house. The Indians steal where they can, both from Northern and from Southern sympathizers. Oh, when will our men folks return?

Nov. 15 - At 5 o'clock this morning someone pounded on my door. They asked for the key to the mill. They said there were 5,000 Confederate troops. There wasn't much in the mill and they paid for what they took. They camped around the mill and made fires with fence rails. Our pigs, ducks and chickens were shot. I was compelled to cook for 18 officers. Hardly had the army moved on, when four rough men came and demanded my saddle. They searched the whole house from attic to cellar and also the smoke-house, and took what they wanted, including carpets, bedding Julius' bath robe and other articles that I had hoped to use for making clothing for the children. They also took what coats and trousers they could find. The poor children clung to me, Elise trembling the most. My hired girl tried to take the articles away from them, but it did no good, so she wept. Julius had put all his household goods in one room and locked it, but they broke it open and took what they could carry. The neighbor Dietrichs were threatened with death.

Nov. 16 - Nobody ventured out on the street today. No one dares to show himself. Toward evening five men and three wagons passed at a gallop. Rhein's and Dietrich's offered to help me hide our goods. We hid meat, lard, sugar, salt, as well as we could. If the robbers find these supplies, we will have to starve. My seven children, including two of Julius', are lying on the beds with all their clothing on except shoes.

Nov. 22 - Day before yesterday our men folks came home unexpectedly. This night I am taking my seven children to Lina's for the night. It is too scary here alone. Our men left again.

Nov. 23 (Sunday) - Lina stayed with me last night, with her children. During the night we heard galloping horses and listened fearfully, trying to learn if they were Northern or Southern troops. A man came to the house in Federal uniform and said he had 600 Union troops and we could rest easily, he would set a guard around the house. We cooked for 13 men and they paid in Northern money. After they had left, some Southern soldiers came. They stopped and rested and ate.

Nov. 24 - Thank God! They have left, after they had stolen everything they could find. The mill looks terrible, everything damaged, but the General had them make new doors for those that they smashed in.
Nov. 26 - Many Southern soldiers in the village today.

Nov. 26 - I spent the entire day making clothing for the seven children. I cut up window curtains and also used a piece of floor carpet and bed-spreads, for it is impossible to secure clothes elsewhere.

Nov. 30 - Freyschlags, who live 25 miles north of us, heard of my situation and invited me to come to them with my children. But I shall remain here as long as we have something to eat. Lina stayed overnight with me, but hardly had she left in the morning than robbers broke into her store and carried away as much as they could. They even took the lock off the door, at least we couldn't find it afterwards. They dropped lots of small things in front of the store.

Dec. 2 - Yesterday our men folks came back. They took a wagon of supplies and went into camp. They would not be safe in the house. Johann's eye is better. It pained him very much when it was infected and he couldn't take care of it. Had to sleep nights in the cold and rain under trees. A neighbor of ours, an American named Williams, and a Southern sympathizer, was among the prisoners in the Federal camp. He had a high fever and asked for Johann. He put his arm about him and said that on the following day all prisoners would have to die. Williams was talking in his delirium and at that time lay on wet straw under the open sky.

Dec. 6 - They stole goods from Fritz's place yesterday.

Dec. 8 - Fritz came home with a pass for him and Johann. Later they went into camp in the woods. Thank God. We want to go to Kansas and from there to St. Louis. But I tremble at the thought of taking the small children at this time of year through a country where we would have to camp every night in the open. I had just set the table for the noonday meal when five rowdy halfbreeds came in and boldly took our places at the table and with much loud laughing ate our meal. They kept their guns with them while they ate. The children were greatly frightened. At first they talked in Cherokee and laughed wickedly. Then they asked in English where our men folks were. I acted as if I did not understand and answered "Ich weiss nicht." and one Indian imitated me. After they left, Lina came over, as pale as death, and said she had heard these halfbreeds say that our men had been killed. I think they were only trying to frighten her.

Dec. 12 - We cannot hold out much longer. During the night, robbers came to Lina's house. What terror! They said they were Union soldiers and Lina gave them what she had. She even showed them her order from General Blunt. However, they called her vile names and demanded money. Gold and silver. They searched the house. One sat down in front of her with his gun while the others searched. The next day, Dec. 13, the same fellows returned, accompanied by about 30 men, took possession of Lina's house and stole what they wanted. Some of them came to my house for food. Toward dusk five fellows came and demanded whiskey. They wouldn't believe me when I told them there was none in the house, and so they searched the house and cellar. I had hit 12 large pieces of burlap which they found. They took seven pieces and left me five. Sometime later they came back to get the burlap and left me only one piece. They took Julius' old rifle, our supply of bread, and some mules. One had my father's long porcelain pipe but I tore it out of his hand. If cold and snow come, we cannot remain longer. We must flee. It is said the Northern troops did not lose the battle, after all. The Southern army passed through on its way to Van Buren.

64

Dec. 14 - Last night a neighbor came and brought us news about our men folks in the Union camp. They are all well. All the women gathered to hear the good news. What tears of joy! Today 500 Pin Indians passed by, with white officers. The children are happy again. They even played the piano.

Dec. 17 - During the night the dogs barked between 12 and 1 o'clock. I was frightened. They stole at the neighbor's house.

Dec. 19 - We are on our way. The axle broke on Fritz's wagon and I am sitting on it, using the opportunity to write in my diary. We had to flee, leaving all possessions behind, but we have our men. I am sorry about sister Mina.

Dec. 20 - Yesterday we reached the Northern camp. The General learned that we had to leave our things behind, so he offered wagon and escort to go and get them but we heard that the Southern troops are again on the march north. Every house and barn and fence around here has been destroyed. Mr. Freyschlag passed by. I called him; he was astonished to see us here. I asked him to get our piano and take it to his home, since he lives off the beaten path of the armies.

— Nany

— H —

(Editor's note: The Hermanns, 19 men, women and children, reached General F.J. Herron's camp at Prairie Grove on Dec. 19, 1862. He gave them an order permitting them to travel with a commissary train to Rolla, Mo. They left Prairie Grove on Dec. 24 and reached Fayetteville the same day, camping at a spring near the north end of that village. Here they spent Christmas Day. Karl Hermann wrote: "The Christ-Child had lost its magic that day. Satan was ruling the land. Looking up at the star-studded sky, our memory saw again the lighted Christmas trees in our Fatherland."

(While camping in Fayetteville, Johann Hermann was taken ill, and for the remainder of the trip had to lie helpless in the wagon. The group reached Springfield on New Year's Eve.

(Progress on the road to St. Louis during February and March 1863 was painfully slow. Tragedy struck in April. Nany, wife of Johann Hermann, and mother of five small children, became ill and six days later she died. Nani's diary ends with this pathetic paragraph, written by her husband:

Washington, Missouri
April 30, 1863

"Here ends the diary of my beloved Nany. At her request I am adding the conclusion. On the 30th of April at 8:30 o'clock in the morning, my poor wife died, after a six days' illness. She called me to her bed and said: 'Jean, tell me the end — I cannot find the words for the end — bring my diary and my pen and ink — you write the end.'")

A CHRISTMAS STORY
by W. J. Lemke

(Reprinted from the Winter 1950 issue of The Arkansas Historical Quarterly, Vol. IX No. 4.)

In the University of Arkansas library there is a privately printed book that gives the history of a group of German families who came to northwest Arkansas in 1850 and founded the village of Hermannsburg (now Dutch Mills) in western Washington County. Prominent among them were two brothers named John and Karl Hermann.

They carried on agriculture, a store, a mill, and other industries. They lived on good terms with their neighbors and were held in high esteem as peaceful and honest folks. They were well on their way to becoming prosperous, when the first signs of approaching civil war appeared. They tried to remain neutral, but were gradually taken to be abolitionists and were considered enemies of the South.

From 1860 to 1862 they were in constant danger from the opposing armies and especially from the thieving and murdering bushwhackers who overran northwest Arkansas. In the fall of 1862 it became evident that continued existence at Hermannsburg was impossible, so the Hermann brothers and their families made ready to flee for safety to St. Louis.

They secured a cavalry escort from General Blunt, the Union commander. They left Cane Hill Dec. 18 in four army wagons, taking only absolute necessities and leaving everything else behind. The group numbered 19, including eleven children from 1 year to 9 years old. The Hermanns reached General Herron's camp at Prairie Grove on Dec. 19. He gave them an order permitting them to travel with a commissary train to Fayetteville and on to Rolla. The following paragraph is a translation from ~~the German diary of Nanni, wife of one of the Hermann brothers:~~ a report of Karl Hermann!

"We left Prairie Grove on Dec. 24 and reached Fayetteville that same day. We camped near a spring at the north end of that village, where we spent Christmas Day. But the Christ-child had lost its magic. Looking up at the star-studded sky on Christmas Eve, our memory saw again the lighted Christmas trees in our distant Fatherland."

Nanni did not live to reach St. Louis. She died ~~on the journey~~ at Washington/60, leaving her husband with ~~three~~ five small children, all born in Washington County, Arkansas.

The spot where these 19 refugees spent their heart-sick Christmas in 1862 was the Big Spring on East Spring street, Fayetteville, which is just across the Town Branch from the Lemke home.

ON CHRISTMAS EVE I SHALL WALK OUT IN MY BACK YARD AND LOOK ACROSS THE RAVINE. AND I SHALL REMEMBER TWO MOTHERS — NANNI HERMANN WITH HER BABIES, SLEEPING IN A WAGON BED IN FAYETTEVILLE, AND MARY WITH HER BABY ASLEEP IN A STABLE IN BETHLEHEM.

—— H ——

BURIED TREASURE AT OLD HERMANNSBURG

(Reprinted from the Washington County Historical Society's "Flashback"
Volume X Number 1)

(Editor's note: Hermannsburg was a Civil War casualty. The families
fled north. Among the last to leave were the Hermanns themselves, with
relatives and friends. This group numbered 19 persons. They left in
December 1862 and spent Christmas Eve in Fayetteville. Events preceding their departure are related in the following account written by
Karl Hermann and published in German after the war. This passage is
translated more or less freely and is much condensed. It contains the
first mention of the Hermanns' buried treasure and sets the scene for
the return of Karl Hermann and his brother-in-law, Julius Wilhelmi, in
1863, to recover the buried gold. This spine-tingling story is Karl
Hermann's own account.)

--- H ---

The Last Days at Hermannsburg

One day a Confederate cavalry troop passed through our village. Out
of curiosity I got on my horse and followed them to Cane Hill. I ob-
served General McCulloch and General Marmaduke riding side by side and
holding a whispered conversation. On my return to Hermannsburg about
noon we heard shooting and the noise of approaching combat. A train of
wagons soon appeared in full gallop, chased by yelling Indians.

I took my family into the cellar. When I got back upstairs I found
an Indian in the door with his gun trained on me. It was a Pin Indian.
He took me to the commander, Colonel Phillips. I told him about Marmaduke's movement.

Because several men of the neighborhood had been killed, I decided
to go north with the Federals. I gave Lina a drawing showing where our
treasure was buried so that she would have means to journey to Missouri in case I failed to return.

As we were preparing to leave, two boys brought information that the
two brothers Fischer, who lived a short distance away on a side road,
had been murdered by the Indians. The group which I joined consisted
of about 1,000 Pin Cherokees under command of white officers. The
Indians had their squaws and babies with them. I joined the crowd of
Confederate captives and non-combatants. My brother John also joined
the exodus.

By morning we reached Camp Babcock, General Blunt's headquarters.
This was in Benton County. We spent some days in the prisoners' camp
and then the army moved to the heights of Cane Hill. I secured per-
mission to go to Hermannsburg and get some of my goods and try to sell
them here. When I returned, soldiers knocked down my tent, wrapping me
in the folds, and stole most of the wares. I suspected the Second Kansas Cavalry but could not identify the culprits. The army then moved
to Prairie Grove and took part in the battle there.

I gave up hope of the Federals furnishing protection for northwest
Arkansas and through friends in St. Louis secured an order from General
Blunt for our passage to Rolla with the necessary escort. We left

Hermannsburg on December 18 with four six-team army wagons and an escort of 100 cavalrymen under Lieutenant Haas. My family occupied one wagon, taking along only absolute necessities and leaving everything else behind.

The total group leaving Cane Hill was nineteen, consisting of Brother John and wife and five children, brother-in-law Julius with two children, myself and wife and three children; a neighbor Dietrich with his wife and one child, and an unmarried Elise Fischer, sister of the two murdered Fischer brothers. The children were from one year to nine years old.

Recovering the Buried Gold

On December 22, 1863, Julius (Wilhelmi) and I (Karl Hermann) obtained an order from General Totten in St. Louis for passage to Fayetteville in order to visit our old home 25 miles south on the road to VanBuren. We left January 3, 1864, by train to Rolla, where we obtained a two-teamed ambulance and several soldiers as escorts.

When we arrived in Springfield, we met our old friend, Freyschlag, (from Fayetteville), who had fled to Springfield to await better times. He reported that the western part of Washington County had been devastated but that the Union troops held Fayetteville. We joined a company of soldiers who were leaving for the outpost of Fayetteville. There we found refuge with our friends, the (Stephen K.) Stone family.

Fayetteville was crowded with refugees of all kinds. From them we learned that neighbors had taken wagon loads of our goods. They had even taken the things which I had hidden between the walls of my house and store. The boiler of the mill and the carding machines had been stolen. The people had fled to Fort Gibson. Blacksmith Nicholas Weber had become insane. Others were hanged or shot for not revealing the hiding place of their money.

Now, only 24 miles from home, it seemed impossible to reach it. During my stay in Fayetteville, a detachment of soldiers, with wagons and axes to get firewood, was attacked and driven in.

I hit on a plan. During the burning of Fayetteville, the court house had been destroyed. Colonel (M. LaRue) Harrison needed lumber and I told him that I had a large supply at Dutch Mills and would be willing to give it to him. He fell in with the idea, and a few days later, seven wagons were prepared and a military escort under Lt. Albright. Lieut. George S. Albright was born Sept. 17, 1841 in Illinois and belonged to the 1st Arkansas Cavalry USA. He was powerfully built, serious for his 23 years, said little, was honest. He was a tolerant man.

I wore a ragged torn overcoat, ragged hat and shoes, and had not shaved for two weeks. I carried a leather saddle-bag on each side, in which I had some goods that were to keep the money from rattling. I also had a space that I took out of Stone's garden, which I carried under my vest with the handle extending down under my boot-tops. Only Brother Julius knew what I was after. The Lieutenant was mounted. The rest of us rode on wagons. The road was very bad and we had to walk up the hills.

L. spade

68

The winter sun was sinking as we crossed the Barren Fork and saw the place where I had spent my best years. While the soldiers camped at the spring, I visited my house. Floors, Walls and stairs had been torn /walls/ up; windows and doors broken; pages from my books and family portraits were scattered over the floor. I went out in the back yard and found it had been dug up. I decided that at least two of my four treasures had not been discovered. The lumber was there. I knew that we would have to spend several days loading the lumber and hoped we would camp here. However, we again resumed our march and when I protested, Lieutenant Albright said: "What, stay in that hole where they can shoot down on us from all sides?"

Disappointed, we went on. Finally, when we had passed a second ford and left the bottoms, we entered the open field of my former neighbor, Evans, about two and a half miles from the mill, where we camped. Saying we wanted to visit our old neighbor, Tennant, who had not fled, we secured a pass from Albright at about 10 o'clock. Julius went ahead because he knew the labyrinth of the river bed. We avoided the Weatherspoon farm house and also avoided the highway. A mile and a half from camp we crossed a road at an open field. It was midnight, pitch dark, when we reached the foot of the hill and saw the house.

Revolver in hand, we waited a while, then I took the spade and began to dig while Julius kept watch on the north side of the house. A door-post still stood in the ground where I had placed it to mark the spot. I loosened the earth and removed the post. I lifted out the heavy stone and the treasure and poured the coins into the saddle-bags. I then tackled the second place, south of the house, and hit a hard object about the size of a gallon jug, but it was a round stone. After a third effort, I found the place and poured the money into the bag. The third place was under a work bench, against the wall of the smoke-house. This was the first treasure I had buried, rather carelessly. It consisted of gold coins in a glass jar. An hour had passed, and now came the most terrible work of this terrible night.

A twelve-foot passage connected the house with the kitchen. The floor of this passage, made of cinders, *covered by flintstones* had been tramped down and was hard to dig in. Changes of the past year, and darkness, prevented my recognizing the hiding place, in which was a jug containing Lina's savings, a silk pocketbook filled with gold, and my neighbors' deposits, and the last money I had taken in in business.

The smokehouse was under a bluff, and all the time I was digging I thought I was being watched from above. I kept on digging, and as I dug more and more of the passage-way I began to fear that it had been discovered. As I kept on digging, my strength left me and I was bathed in perspiration. I did not notice the approaching dawn. Nor an approaching thunderstorm. It began to rain. Julius whispered that the sound of my digging could be heard through the whole valley. I threw the spade away and dug with bowie knife and hands in the sharp stones of the floor until my fingers bled. Julius insisted that we would have to leave, and that the saddle-bag was already too heavy to carry. If I did not stop digging he would leave me. I returned to consciousness, I asked for just a few more minutes and then covered the ground with branches and leaves, hid the spade, and followed Julius. I had no idea of the weight of the money. Julius carried it on his shoulder.

When we reached the deserted home of the miller Kraft, we heard a metallic noise. Figuring sixty pounds for $1,000 in silver, the weight was more than 200 pounds without the gold. We took off a fence-rail, hung the bag in the middle, and each carried an end of it on his shoulder. We climbed down the bluffs and crossed the Barren Fork. The water was up to our waists.

The night was pitch dark. Our faces and hands were scratched. We heard the water at the second crossing of the Barren Fork. I did not see the edge of the bluff and stepped over and fell. The breath was knocked out of me. Julius stopped when he felt the bag disappear. I still carry the scars of that fall on my hands.

We hid in the woods until we heard sounds in the camp, and when the rain and lightning increased, we hid in a hollow tree. When it was light, Julius took the bag on his shoulder and we entered the camp and put the bag in the wagon.

In a pouring rain, we went down Cane Hill. I climbed onto the piano box. I carried the small glass jar of gold in my inside pocket. As I climbed on the wagon, the glass fell and gold pieces rolled all over the road. All the wagons stopped, and the soldiers helped me hunt the gold. We found my piano in a house near Boonsboro. The family refused to give it up, but Albright ordered several soldiers into the house and the piano was placed in the box on top of the treasure. While camping that night, Lieut. Albright whispered to me, "My boys found out that you have money on you. I trust none of them. You had better stay close to me tonight." The Lieutenant ordered all soldiers to sleep in a farm house. I slept with my eyes and ears open. A couple of shots were heard outside, but the Lieutenant took no notice and nothing happened.

Without further adventure we reached Fayetteville at two o'clock in the afternoon. The piano was unloaded at the Stone home and the men commented on the weight of the piano. Next day I packed the piano, removing the legs, the iron piano stool, and packed them with the money and a lot of books belonging to a woman living with Freyschlag who was going to Missouri. The books were visible through the cracks in the box and would explain the weight of the box. The Stones suspected what was going on. They probably learned through Albright, who later married the charming daughter of the house.

Julius left the next day for Missouri. I received $45 for the lumber and a permit from Colonel Harrison to join a company of soldiers going toward Cane Hill. The evening of the next day we camped three miles from Boonsboro.

The officer gave me an escort of eight Indians, to visit my home seven miles away. When we reached the spring I told the Indians to wait for me, went to the house, found the/space and began to dig. Time passed and the excavation became larger and larger. I did not want to leave until I was certain the treasure was not there. As I straightened up to take a deep breath, my glance fell on the house of my neighbor. I saw a dark figure, made out a man who was watching me and holding a gun. I recognized him as one of the Pins who had crept up to watch what I was doing. I knew now that if I found the treasure

L space

70

I would probably be killed. I threw the spade away, covered the ground with branches, walked over to the Indian and told him that I was looking for a key that I had lost. He probably didn't believe me.

We returned to Fayetteville. The $45 I got for the lumber, I paid to Freyschlag for the horse I used to go out on this trip. The trip from Fayetteville to Rolla took two weeks. I slept on the piano box.

(Editor's note: From Rolla, Karl Hermann took the train to St. Louis. Descendants of the Hermanns believe that the recovered gold financed the family's return to Germany and the care of Johann Hermann's motherless children. The mother, Nanny, died in April 1863 at Washington, Mo., while on the flight from Old Hermannsburg to St.Louis.)

RESEARCH NOTES
by W.J.Lemke

I got so interested inthe story of OldHermannsburg (now Dutch Mills) in our county that I probably made myself a nuisance to kinsmen of the Hermanns, especially Prof.W.E.Meyer of State College,Pa., and Wolfgang Gscheidlen of Stuttgart, Germany, with both of whom I have carried on a correspondence covering eight or ten years.

There were things I did not understand. For instance, their being able to get along with the Indians, who lived just a mile or two west of the Hermanns, and with the Negroes, who must have been a completely new experience for the German immigrants. Yet the Germans were able to teach at least one Negro servant to speak German. And John Hermann and other members of the family picked up quite a bit of Cherokee. The following quotes are from letters from Mr.Wolfgang Gscheidlen:

The Indians
The Indians of the region belonged to the Cherokee, Sioux and Blackfoot tribes. Elise cites the first 6 numbers of the Indian language: sago, tale, soe, nake, sudderle. The Sioux were, I think, Osage Indians. There have been only a few Blackfoots in the region. Johann Hermann supplied the Indians — they spoke English with him; Karl learned some Indian words, such as flour and other goods. The Indians helped him and Julius Wilhelmi with felling trees, etc.

The Negroes
Johann Hermann hired a Negro girl (Martha) in September 1851: "She was young, dirty, enormously wasteful and had all the other faults of ill-educated Negroes." She ran away, but he got her back after two weeks. Nanni Hermann wrote 25.7.1852: "Our hired Negro-girl is not very quick and therefore I have to help much, that the dinner at due time comes upon the table." Johann Hermann hired, at the beginning of the year 1852 a Negro family (man, wife, two children), and had to give 160 dollars each year. Karl bought a Negro girl Melinda for 900 dollars in gold. She was young, soon learned the German language. "Besides", Karl wrote, "she increased my property by children not wanted". In August 1862 Melinda was kidnapped by a Negro who also stole his master's horses and covers.

71

Other details that I investigated concerned locations in the Dutch Mills area a hundred years ago. I wanted to know just where the German immigrants lived, where the Freyschlag mill was located, everything about the Barren Fork river and the Whittaker branch, and especially about the buried gold that the Hermanns didn't find but that legend says was used to pay for a farm after the war. Regarding the Freyschlag mill, here is a quote from a letter from Mr. Gscheidlen of Germany:

Freyschlag's Mill

You cite two possible sites for the Freyschlag mill — north of Lincoln, about 8 miles from Hermannsburg, and on Clear Creek, about 12 miles off. Johann Hermann wrote 10.7.1850 to his brother Wilhelm at Lyon: "I am already more than two months with a German named Freyschlag. Mr. Freyschlag has a mill that I repaired and put in many improvements. In some days, I will establish 12 miles from here (from the Freyschlag mill) a cotton factory and will take care of it till I begin my own business. The proprietor is always absent. I am getting 40 dollars each month and food for me and my horse. Below: care of Mr. Freyschlag, Fayetteville, Washington County, North America, State of Arkansas." That means that Freyschlag's mill must have been near Fayetteville. But Fayetteville is 25 miles distant from Dutch Mills. Nanni Hermann wrote 30.11.62: "Freyschlags are dwelling 25 miles north of here, off the road, therefore not so disturbed."

> (Editor's note: After considerable research, I have come to the conclusion that the Freyschlag mill of the 1850s was located on Clear Creek, at the site of the later Pegram mill.)

The log house of Johann Hermann

In 1946 Mrs. Anita Hermann Bilharz sent a picture of the log house to my sister Hedi, who gave it to me. Anita wrote: "It is a cabin on a hillside, built of logs. The house looks unpretentious."

On my map I show this log-house at the eastern side of the Whitaker branch. But Mrs. Leach wrote at this place "Old Hermann site" on her sketch which she sent me. But she writes of the site on the west hill "where I live and I think where Julius Wilhelmi lived." That must be a mistake, because Julius lived on the hill north of Karl. Mrs. Leach wrote me 22.4.64: "I am living where my mother told me the first frame house was built. It is on the west hill overlooking the little stream".

Mr. Gscheidlen writes: "You (W.J.L.) wrote me 9.10.64: "Jack Reed says his family lived in a house that stood on the site of Mrs. Leach's home at Dutch Mills, which stood on the site of John Hermann's first log house."

Johann Hermann wrote to his mother 24.8.1851: "The house we are living in is small, 15-16 feet the inner room, built only of logs, with a fore part, the half of it shut in by boards and serving as a kitchen; the other half of the fore part is open, serving as a place of residence during the hot time of the day and as a dining room. The house is surrounded by the creek on three sides and around it are tall trees".

> (Editor's note: There is no doubt in my mind that Johann Hermann's first log house was on the site of Mrs. Leach's present home (1965) and the place where the Reed family lived. The photo appears in this booklet. WJL)

MARKER ERECTED AT OLD HERMANNSBURG 1963 by the Washington County Historical Society and descendants of the pioneers.

LIBERTY BAPTIST CHURCH at DUTCH MILLS

The present-day Baptist church that stands atop the hill at Dutch Mills. Behind the church is the Weber cemetery, in which are buried the first two Welhelmis of the German *L. Wilhelmis* colony. At the time of their burial this was "in the forest." It is now a well-kept graveyard and many of the post-war pioneers are buried here.

Photos by W. J. Lemke

73

A WAR-TIME LETTER OF FRANZ WILHELMI
Captain in the 17th Regiment of Missouri Volunteers, addressed to his sister Marie (Mrs. Greiner) in Germany.

(Translated by Wolfgang Gscheidlen)

25th February 1862

My wife sent me your letter of November and I am glad to learn from it that at least my brother and my sister are well and in good health. What is brother Wilhelm? clergyman or professor? Since I am out of touch with my loved ones, I must write to you directly to hear from you. Otherwise it was father who informed me.

Just imagine, I am sitting here in my tent, only 36 miles or a day's journey to Hermannsburg but I can tell you nothing of our family. An army, three times as big as ours, stands between us. I have found out by asking that the two Hermanns with their families were well in December. The man didn't know father or Julius and Eberle, because they were not yet there when the man lived there. (My annotation: Franz's father died Sept. 10, 1861.) He was the same man from whom Jean Hermann bought the place 10 years ago. I hope to hear more about them and will let you know.

My brother-in-law L.Schmidt is Sergeant in my company and H.Schmitt, now wounded, is head gunman, chief of piece in the 1st Missouri Artillery Regiment. Amil Blumer, one of my corporals, as well as George Landfried, brother of my brother Julius' wife, who died too early. (Annotation: E. Blumer was killed at Chattanooga, Tenn.; G. Landfried at Vicksburg, Miss. Luise, wife of Julius, had died in 1861.)

I did get the last news of my family some weeks ago, because I was on the move. My last experiences I can tell you only briefly. On the 11th of June 1861 I entered the service of the US Reserve for three months. After this time, during which I had only to protect bridges and railroads, I entered again as Captain of the Western Turner Rifle Regiment, the 17th Missouri, in active service for three years. We marched from St. Louis to Sedalia, from there to Springfield where we with 30,000 men intended to attack the enemy. But they, 50,000 men strong, retired. Fremont, our famous general, was called back and we had to retreat without a fight and took winter quarters at Rolla, Mo. That means, we pitched our tents 110 miles to the east; there is no thought of being billeted in houses.

From there, we had to start for Lebanon on the 15th of January and on the 8th of February to Springfield. We were a daring band of 10,000 men with 48 cannons. Ten miles from Springfield, we met the enemy's army of 15,000 men and 54 cannons. We pursued them for six days from Missouri deep into Arkansas, now and then killing some and taking more of them prisoner. Daily our advance guard fired at their rear guard but we could not come to a pitched battle, the enemy always retiring to the Arkansas army. Now we are waiting here for reinforcements and for our baggage that could not be moved so fast towards us, and therefore some of us, e.g. my company and I, have been without tents and blankets for nearly 14 days and have hardly been provided with the most necessary victuals. With the ground as our bed, the cloak as our cover, thus we camped around the fires at night and roasted our beef-steaks on sticks. By day we marched often 25-30 miles, now in mud up to our ankles, then again over hard-frozen ground, as the change of the local climate brings it about, always prepared for attack.

Although we officers have more privileges than even the soldiers in Germany, e.g. comfortable tents, servants, horses and so on, I shared most of the hardships in order to set a good example to my men. I had my attendant ride while I marched myself. Now we again have provisions and we need not take away every eatable from the farmers. We have col-lected many horses and wagons and so on, so that we officers of the infantry and of the riflemen are nearly all on horseback, we who ought to be on foot.

We try to avoid the terrors of the civil war, so far as possible, but we cannot prevent all atrocities. In Bentonville, a flourishing small town 3 miles from here, a soldier of a patrol was shot from a house and killed; another stoned and killed. Then the furious soldiers laid fire to the town and some 20 houses burned down. Also, poison plays a part and a captain of cavalry died the day before yesterday. But I am far from asserting that this was done by our regular enemies of the Southern army; it is fanatical marauders who make use of such weapons.

General Price and his gang — we are ashamed to fight against them - have now been driven out ofMissouri and I hope that we are going to be opposed to the regular army before long. It's a pity that the latter is in the neighborhood of Hermannsburg, 7 miles toward us. In case we should get there, I shall have the opportunity to protect our families. I have already spoken with General Sigel about it. But I hope that the enemy then will go to Fort Smith, because our reinforcements must arrive within the next few days and the enemy then will not offer us a battle in open field.

By the newspapers you will see that also in the other states our arms have been victorious, and so I hope the South will soon have to yield and I shall return to civil life with full honor, from a status that I have chosen because of patriotism, that the indifference and indecision of our government made impalatable to us. Had men like Fremont and Sigel been placed at the top, patriotism would not have changed into rheumatism and the war would have been finished a long time ago. To resign now would throw the suspicion of cowardice on us. Therefore I shall help to fight out the struggle, which I can do with good conscience with regard to my family. My wife would obtain 30 dol-lars monthly for life, if anything should happen to me. Really, in financial respects, Uncle Sam is very honest and does pay me now monthly for my forced inaction 131½ dollars.

(Translator's annotation: Franz Wilhelmi was born 18 Feb. 1827 at Stebbach near Eppingen, Germany. His father was Wilhelm Wilhelmi. One of his brothers was Julius. A sister Nanni married Johann Hermann, who founded Hermannsburg, Washington County, Ark. Franz Wilhelmi emigrated in 1849 and went to Gray's Summit, Franklin County, Mo., where he found-ed the "Wilhelmi Farm", now called Hardeman farm. Later he went to Washington, Mo., where he died 28 January 1883. He was a Captain in General Curtis' army and in July 1864 became Major in General Sigel's army. He returned to civil life in September 1864.)

--- H ---

WILHELM HERMANN

Wilhelm Hermann, the father of the two Hermanns who are usually named as the founders of the German settlement of Hermannsburg in Washington County, Arkansas 115 years ago (Johann Heinrich Hermann and Karl Friedrich Hermann), was born 14.6.1776 at Bonfeld near Heilbronn, Germany. He died 29.5.1848 at Heidelberg. He was an apothecary at Mannheim, where he operated the "Mohren-Apotheke."

Wilhelm Hermann married (1st) Johanna Dorothea von Fischer, who was born 1787, died 1812, a Catholic. Out of this marriage he had a son Wilhelm, born 8.1.1805 at Mannheim; died 25.1.1876 in Lyon. He had gone to Lyon in 1823 to became head clerk of a big bank. He retired in 1865. He married Julie Marie Pierrette Davallon, born Lyon 9.9.1815; died 7.12.1866 at Lyon. (Wilhelm was a Protestant). A daughter Matilde, born 11.9.1808 (Catholic); died 15.11.1881 at Heidelberg. She married Christian Heinrich Glaser, receiver-general at Sinsheim, who died 2.6.1833. *[Children: Alice (* 25.3.1838, † 7.4.1899, ∞ Joseph Bonnel, professeur de mathématiques), Jules (* 27.3.1840, commis négociant, ∞ Louise Kiffler; Adolphe (* 18.7.1850, négociant, ∞ Clémence Chamard)]*

Wilhelm Hermann married 2nd on 12.9.1812 at Bensheim, Elise Glaess, born 3.9.1792 in Bensheim; died 15.1.1858 at Lauda. She was Catholic. They had six children, the last Heinrich died as a child. The others:

1. Elisabeth, born 1814. Catholic. Died 29.6.1843. She married August Halberstadt, an apothecary at Camberg who died 1862.

2. Amalie, born 7.4.1819; died Mannheim 5.11.1891. Catholic. She married Philipp Schmitt, an architect of Mannheim who was born 8.5.1809 and died 22.10.1876. Amalie had no children, but brought up the five children of her brother, Johann Heinrich, after his wife Nanni died in Washington, Missouri.

3. Johann Heinrich, the founder of Old Hermannsburg in Washington County, Arkansas. (See his biography on another page.) He was a Protestant and married Nanni Wilhelmi.

4. Karl Friedrich, Protestant. He married Lina Wilhelmi, sister of Nanni. (His biography elsewhere in this book.)

5. Eduard, born 19.12.1829 at Mannheim; died 29.1.1889 at Heidelberg. Protestant. He was an apothecary at Kehl on the Rhine. He married 22.11.1855 to Anna Graul, born 20.11.1832 at Worms; died 17.3.1909 at Heidelberg. Eduard is the "lustige Bruder Wattl" ("the Merry brother W.") of whom Nanni wrote in her letters. *[4 children: Kathinka ∞ apothecary at Stuttgart Pastor Moerike; Wilhelm (apothecary at Kehl); Fritz (chief-burgomaster at Offenburg, then Wiesbaden) and Amalie ∞ Adolf Hoffmann, apothecary at Mannheim.]*

Family information from

Wolfgang Gscheidlen, Stuttgart, Germany

CHILDREN OF JOHANN HERMANN AND NANNI WILHELMI

The four children of Mr. and Mrs. John Hermann were born at Old Hermannsburg, now Dutch Mills, Washington County, Arkansas. They were:

1. Elise, born 26.4.1853 at Hermannsburg

2. 1. Minna, born 4.11.1854 at Hermannsburg; died 11.4.1934. She was baptized at Mannheim 27.10.1867 by the Rev. E.O.Schellenberg. She married 12.9.1877 at New York to Wilhelm Grevel, whom she first saw aboard ship when her father brought her back to the USA in 1873. She adopted Ada, who married Fred Acker, a New York insurance man. Ada had two sons: Grevel and Wilfred.

3. 2. Wilhelm, born 11.10.1856 at Hermannsburg; baptized 27.10.1867 at Mannheim. Dr. Spiegelhalter, a friend of his father, brought Wilhelm to the USA in 1871. He became a doctor of dentistry in St. Louis. He married in 1881 Johanna Bang, was divorced, had three children: Johanna, born St.Louis 24.9.1882; Ella, born St.Louis 3.5.1884; and Ada, born St.Louis 7.2.1887. Wilhelm married a second time at Frankfort-on-Main.

4. 3. Julie, born 17.2.1858 at Hermannsburg; baptized 27.10.1867 at Mannheim in Germany. She was married to Christian Graff of New York and died in 1929. Her daughter Amelie, born 3.6.1883, married a man named Parsons of Long Island, N.Y. Julie also had a son Willy, born Oct. 1884 who married Marie —— and had two daughters, Virginia, born April 1909 and Elizabeth.

5. 4. Oskar, born 10.12.1860 at Hermannsburg; baptized 27.10.1867 at Mannheim. His father brought him back to the USA in 1873. In 1879 he was a student in the mechanical engineering school in St.Louis and became an electrical engineer at Camden, N.J. After 1892 he had a farm and peach orchard at Cuthbert, Ga. He lost his right hand in an accident. He married 15.3.1885 Sarah Bishop, born 24.2.1864 at Big Sandy, Texas. He had six children: Johann Wilhelm, born 11.10.1886 at Greely, Colo.; Oscar Julius, born 22.4.1887 at St. Louis; Minna Julia, born 6.10.1889 at Orange, N.J.; Ida Bishop, born 19.6.1891 at Gloucester, N.J.; Walter (E.J.) born 13.3.1894 at Cuthbert, Ga.; and Eloise.

Family information furnished by
Wolfgang Gscheidlen of Stuttgart, Germany

CHILDREN of KARL FR. HERMANN and LINA WILHELMI

1. Heinrich W., born 9.6.1855 at Hermannsburg, Ark.; died 18.8.1928 in St.Louis. He studied medicine at Heidelberg from 19.10.1879 and also at the University at Wien. Became a doctor at St. Louis. He married 18.11.1896 to Linda Hofmann, born 18.11.1869; died 13.12.1934. She was the daughter of Ernest G. Hofmann and Clara Steinwender. They had two daughters: Vera Dorothea, born 10.1.1898 in St. Louis (she married Edward Cox), and Margerite who married Sheridan Loy at St. Louis.

2. Edward A., born 28.12.1856 at Hermannsburg, Ark.; died 12.6.1941 in St.Louis. He was a civil engineer in St.Louis. He married 30.4.1896 to Florence Pitzman, born 12.1.1869, daughter of Julius Pitzman and Emma Tittman. They had a son, Charles Edward, born 20.12.1901, who married Jesse Tyler.

3. Louis C., born 13.7.1859 at Hermannsburg, Ark; died 4.3.1932 in St. Louis. As a boy he attended school at Heidelberg, Germany. He became secretary-treasurer of the Hermann & Koenitzer Oak Leather Co. of St. Louis. He married 16.10.1889 to Ida Helmle, born 17.3.1868 in Spring- field, Ill., the daughter of Carl A. Helmle and Marie Flesche. Their children were:

   a) Marie, born 31.8.1890; married Richard Holekamp; had five sons and two daughters.

   b) Friedrich (Fred) Albert, born 6.8.1892; married Evelyn Ringen; two children.

   c) Alice
   + 14.12.1895
   ∞ to Milton
   Kahle
   c) Anita Stephanie, born 6.10.1896; married Oscar W. Bilharz, a   *↳ Chicago*
   mining engineer at Baxter Springs, Kans. Bilharz prepared pedi-   *24.9.1972*
   gree charts for the Bilharz and Hermann families. His wife Anita
   in 1946 sent the photo of the Hermanns' first log house at Her-
   ↳ to mannsburg. To Wolfgang Gscheidlen. The Bilharzes had four children.
   Birk × 1923 mechanical engineer; Anita Stephanie × 1925, ∞ Baxter Springs 12.6.1948 to Charles Wells; Karrain × 1928;
   Ted × 1931

   e) Norma
   + 21.9.
   1900
   ∞ to William
   Brown
   Gerhardt
4. Alice, born 16.1.1869 in St.Louis; married 7.1.1897 to George Engels- mann, a St. Louis merchant who was born 13.8.1864 in Washington, D.C.; and died after 1941. They had two sons: George (who married Imogene *↳ × 9.11.1882* *↳ ∞ 8.6.* Lockett, and William Hermann, who married Dorothy Louise Burg. Alice *↳ 12.4.1931* Hermann Engelsmann died 6.5.1944 in St.Louis.

5. Lina, born 7.10.1871 in St.Louis; married Louis Hofmann (brother of Linda who married Heinrich Hermann). They had three sons: Walter who married Virginia Niedringhaus (divorced) and 2nd Dorothy Becker; Carl who married Dorothy Spiegelhalter; and Stanley, twin brother of Carl, *↳ Ernest* who married Lucia Weaver (divorced).

6. Amalie Julie, born 7.5.1876 St.Louis; married 8.5.1901 to Arthur E. Leussler. They lived in St.Louis and had son, Arthur Julian, born *↳ 26.4.1935* 14.1.1902 who married Valerie Cale.

Family information from Wolfgang Gscheidlen
of Stuttgart, Germany.

A. WILHELM WILHELMI

Father of Nanni (Mrs. Johann Hermann) and Lina (Mrs. Karl Hermann) of Old Hermannsburg, Washington County, Arkansas.

Abraham <u>Wilhelm</u> Wilhelmi was born at Heidelberg, Germany 27.1.1790; died at Hermannsburg, Arkansas 7.10.1861 at 3 p.m. He is buried in the Weber cemetery at Dutch Mills, Washington County, Arkansas.

L 3.30

He served a number of churches in Germany, beginning in 1813. On 23.3.1850 he got a furlough for a year and left Mannheim for America on 15.4.1850. He left Germany with his wife and his daughters (Nanni and Lina). His sons, Julius and Franz, had emigrated the previous year and were living in Missourinin 1849.

L Missouri in

Before he left Mannheim, the Rev. Wilhelmi made a visit with the Rev. Michael Nuessle at nearby Sandhofen, whose wife was a sister of his. (She was Luise Wittich, born 9.9.1809 at Mauer; had married 19.5.1829 to Michael Nuessle, born 20.10.1799.)

L +Rueppur 14.12.1888

Wilhelm Wilhelmi married 11.11.1817 to Johanna Wittich, born Mannheim 15.10.1792; died 7/8.1852 at the Wilhelmi Farm near Grays Summit, Missouri. Wilhelm and Johanna Wilhelmi became the parents of eight children. The 7th child, Friedrich, born 15.2.1830, died in infancy.)

1. Marie - born 8.8.1818 at Stebbach; died New York 1894. She came to the USA in 1867. She married 27.6.1839 Heinrich Greiner, born near Offenburg 27.1.1801; died 1.6.18581 Their children:

    L Allmannsweier

    a) Otto, born 14.12.1841; died St. Louis 8.11.1887. He was a medical doctor and practiced in New Orleans. He married 30.4.1866 Magdalene Zoeller, born 20.10.1842, daughter of Colonel Zoeller at Karlsruhe.

    b) Heinrich Wilhelm Eberhard, born 23.8.1847, chief conductor at New York; married Margarete Zoeller, sister of Magdalene Goeller Zoeller.

    c) Mathilde .... , ∞ .... to Theodore Schulz, New York

Wilhelm, born 4.11.1819 Stebbach, + 15.5.1877

2. Wilhelm Mathilden Wilhelm 1819 at Theobach Schild 1851 at New York at Brudersdorf in Mecklenburg. He held various pastoral charges (Lutheranan) beginning in 1850. He was married three times. Out of his first marriage with Marie Lauter he had three children, who soon died. There were no children by his second marriage, to Marie Sabel. He then married 10.10.1850 Rosine La Roche, born Basel 6.10.1829; died Rostock 23.10.1910. By his third wife he had eight children, of whom the second child died in infancy. The *L Jonathan* others:

    L 23.11.1851

    a) Heinrich, born 23.111.1851; died 16.2.1919. He was pastor at Hamburg and had a son Heinrich, born 25.4.1888 who also became pastor at Hamburg and is still living there.

    b) Ludwig, born 14.1.1855; died 15.4.1923, who was pastor of a number of churches in Mecklenburg.

c) Axel, born 13.11.1857; died 20.6.1928. Was a doctor of medicine. His daughter Martha (died 1945) had married Dr. Med. Justus Hoff, who died 1933. The daughter of Martha, Ursula, married Prof.Dr. Wolfgang Stechow and is living with her daughters Babbara and Nicola and son Hans Axel in Ober-lin, Ohio. A sister of Martha, Gertrud, who married Meinhard Jacoby, artist-painter, is also living in Oberlin, Ohio and collecting information about the Hermann and Wilhelmi famil-ies in the US.

d) Paul, born 15.10.1858; died before 1938.

e) Helene, born 8.3.1863; died 28.3.1940 in Rostock, married the Rev. Friedrich Voss.

(f) Marie, born 4.8.1867; died 9.7.1893 in Paris, Married lst Friedrich Voss, later husband of her sister.

g) Karl, born 16.10.1871; died 21.11.1944, at Illzach bei Muehlhausen, Elsass. He was a lieutenant and a merchant.

3. Minna, born 13.4.1821; died St.Louis 17.2.1881. She married 15.4.1845 to the Rev. Johann Jakob Eberle, pastor at Palmbach near Durlach. After emigrating to America, they lived first in Missouri and then at Hermannsburg, Washington County, Arkansas. They had eight children, the first three born in Germany:
   a) Marie Franziska, born 18.2.1846; died 18.4.1886
   b) Hermann Friedrich, born 3.9.1847; died 30.5.1887
   c) Julius Heinrich, born 12.3.1849; died 24.10.1872
   d) Wilhelm, born 23.5.1850; died 11.5.1869
   e) A son born 1852 (?) at the Wilhelmi Farm
   f), g), h) - No information

4. Julius who married in 1852 to Luise Landfried. Living 1852 in Franklin County, Mo., with his parents and brothers and sisters. One brother was George, who was a corporal with Franz Wilhelmi and was killed in front of Vicksburg, Miss.) Nanni in her letter to Johann Hermann's mother 22.9.1852 said that Julius had built a good double-log house. In 1873 he was notary public at Washington, Mo. and certificated the death of his sister Nanni.

5. Nanni, born 2.8.1825 at Stebbach. Karl Hermann wrote about Nanni: "In Johann's wife Nanni I met a model of education in a parsonage. She was rather short than of a tall stature. She had a juvenile look. Her face revealed always a happy mood. She was always good-natured. When her full-sounding song was warbling through the refreshing air of the evening, I forgot the hardships of life on the frontier." A letter of Good Friday 1850 to her cousin Mina at Ensheim still exists. Nanni wrote that they would emigrate the week after Easter. This letter is in my possession; Lina also wrote to Mina, her cousin, on the back side of the letter. When they were at Sandhofen with Michael Nuessle, Nani and Lina went through the gardens singing "Wir winden Dir den Jungfernkranz" (We are weaving for you the bridal wreath), arm in arm. Michael Nuessle's youngest son Adolf, born 3.3.1843, later married the daughter of Nanni Hermann, Elise.
An album of Nanni's still exists (in the possession of Liselotte Nuessle, married Kosbahn at Muenchen, granddaughter of Elise). In this

album ten of Nanni's girl friends have written; there are silhouettes, water-colors and drawings. Father Wilhelmi and mother have written poems in the album.

(silhouette)

Nanni gave to Elise a golden brooch, containing two photos of Johann. The brooch has a ring set with a pearl on a coronet; at the sides two smaller pearls on coronets; below a small ruby in a flower. Elise gave this brooch to her daughter Minna (my mother) at her confirmation. Now my sister/Ilsa has this brooch.

Elise

Nanni died 30.4.1863 at 5 o'clock in the morning, according to death certificate signed by Dr. F.C.Schweikart. As cause of death the Doctor gives "congestive fever." She died at Washington, Mo. She was buried 1.5.1863 at Wildey's cemetery. Witnesses who signed the certificate were G. Muench and Gert Goebel. Julius Wilhelmi acted as notary. The certificate still exists in my possession.

(Other biographical facts and names of Nanni's children are given on an earlier page of this genealogical section.)

6. Franz, born at Stebbach near Eppingen, Baden, 18.2.1827; died 28.1.1883. He was a land-surveyor and in 1849 went to Missouri with his brother Julius to establish a farm near Grays Summit in Franklin County, the so-called "Wilhelmi Farm" (now the Hardeman farm). In 1853 he had a contract to survey the building of the Pacific railroad through the "Wilhelmi-Farm." Franz married at Bauschlott 21.2.1850 Alwine Schmidt, born at Bruchsal 17.1.1830. She died 3.2.1883. She was the daughter of Michael Schmidt, district judge at Heidelberg, and of Johanna Buerck. A brother of Alwine, L. Schmidt, was sergeant-major in the company with Franz. Franz became a Captain in the Union army 11.6.1861 and served under General Curtis in 1862 and under General Sigel in 1864 until he was discharged in September 1864. Five children:

Anna, Max, Clara, Minna and Alwine,

a) Anna, born at Labadie, Mo. 2.7.1851; died 14 Jan.(?). She married 19.2.1869 to Heinrich Grappe of Hamburg, Iowa. Their daughter Helene was born 5.12.1870; married 20.8.1904 to Ide Friedrich Husterhagen. A daughter/Annette born 7.7.1905. She married 2nd Louis Schwartz 11.3.1874, a portrait painter of New York. Had daughter Olga who married Frank Rogers. She married 3rd to Johann Jungbauer, a New York furrier.

L of Helene

great grandparents

7. Lina, born 17.3.1834. She married Karl F. Hermann. (Biography and names of her children on an earlier page.)

(All family information in these records from
Wolfgang Gscheidlen of Stuttgart, Germany.)

82

MAIN STREET, DUTCH MILLS, ARK. 1910
This is the main street of Dutch Mills, Ark. 50 years ago, and 50 years after the Hermanns had left it. The store at the right occupies the approximate site of Karl Hermanns store in 1854.

ANOTHER OLD MILL AT DUTCH MILLS
The mill pictured above was a successor to the Hermanns' mill of a half century earlier. It was located on the same site, but steam power had replaced water power from the Whittaker Branch. This mill was destroyed by fire in 1925 and as of today (1965) there is no mill at Dutch Mills.

--EPILOGUE--
1976

To follow the only male descendents known to bear the Hermann name in this country.

Karl Friedrich and his wife, Lina, moved their family of three boys and three girls to St. Louis from Hermannsburg in 1863.

Frederick Albert, son of Louis Charles, grandson of Karl Friedrich, has two sons, both graduates in Mechanical Engineering at Princeton University.

1. The oldest, Robert Ringen, is President of Standard Container Company, St. Louis. He has one son, Robert Ringen, Jr., a graduate of Princeton University.

2. The youngest, Frederick Albert, Jr., is President of the Hermann Oak Leather Company, St. Louis (a leather tannery operation founded in 1881 by Louis Charles Hermann). He has two sons: Lawrence Shepley, a graduate of Princeton University and Frederick Albert, III, an undergraduate at the University of Virginia.

These, then, are five generations from the year 1851 when the Hermann brothers set up housekeeping at Hermannsburg in Washington County, Arkansas, now know as Dutch Mills, Arkansas.

This is the romantic tale of the Germann colony that settled in our country 114 years ago and was driven out by civil war.

Supplement: Children of Johann Hermann and Nanni Wilhelm

1. Elise Hermann was the first child of Johann Heinrich Hermann and of Nanni born Wilhelmi. She was born in Hermannsburg the 26.th of April 1853, baptized (1855?) by her grandfather Wilhelm Wilhelmi. Elise died at Wiesloch,Baden (Germany) the 11th of September 1920, 12.30 o'clock. She married Tuesday, 18.11.1873 at Mannheim Adolf Nuessle (born 3.3.1843 at Sandhofen-now suburb of Mannheim-; he died 25.3.1911 at Mannheim.He was 1885 Oberfoerster, 1899 he became Forstmeister,dwelt in the castle in Mannheim). The ceremony was performed by the father of Adolf, Michael,reverend, in the Trinitatiskirche. Michael Nuessle was married with Luise Wittich, sister of Johanna Wittich(married with Wilhelm Wilhelmi).
Elise had 3 children:
1) Otto: born Monday, 31.8.1874 at Schriesheim,Baden,+ 26.3.1914 at Mannheim(by an accident).He was engineer,drove the first cars and bicycles.He was inspector of the Company of Baden in controlling boilers.He married 6.4.1906 at Kaiserslautern Marie Krafft,born 5.12.1880 at Westhofen, + 2.12.1966 at Muenchen.She was a daughter of the rotary August Krafft(born Zweibruecken 17.8.1850, + Westhofen 14.3.1883) and of Johanna Gerle (born Kaiserslautern 15.10.1858, + Kaiserslautern23.11. 1921). Otto had three children:
a) Liselotte: born Karlsruhe 24.1.1908, + Muenchen 10.4.1971 (cancer of the connective tissue).Played piano like a pianist.Married Muenchen 6.4.1936 to Herbert Kosbahn,born Muenchen 31.10.1909,"Diplomwirtschafter" with "Brandl's Keimdiät" at Augsburg(= certificated economist).He was a son of Carl Kosbahn,"Zeichner"(designer),born Berlin 2.5.1879, + Muenchen, and of Luise Ziehe,born 24.4.1877 Lindenberg n ear Luckenwalde,+ Muenchen. Herbert Kosbahn married 2)1976 to ...
Liselotte had 3 children:
1) Klaus,born 10.6.1937 Muenchen.Since 1959 member of the "Muenchner Kammerorchester",playing violin,since about 1966 tenor violin.
2) Wolfgang,born 28.1.1940 Muenchen. Dr.chem at the TU at Muenchen.Plays tenor violin and piano very well.He married at Roellingsen,Westfalen 1.1.1964 Margret Tillmanns, born Roellingsen 9.4.1936,violin teacher. Children: Annette,born Muenchen 28.8.1965, and Karolin, born Muenchen 23.10.1967.
3) Gerda,born Miesbach 23.5.1945. Became singer and actress at the theatre of Hannover.   (Cancer of the larynx)
b) Walter: born Villingen 28.4.1909, + Buenos Aires 29.7.1975. Became mechancian for cars.He emigrated,was living since 1951 on the Estancia La Marianita,Condarco, Provincia Buenos Aires,Argentina.He married Kleve (Rheinland) 28.10. 1946 Ilse Letzke,born Kleve 26.1.1916,daughter of Erich Letzke(born Kleve 25.1.1888,+ Kleve Sept.1944),"Prokurist", and of Margarete Richter(born Chemnitz 13.10.1890,+Kleve 31.3.1965).Walter was divorced 12.5.1958 at Muenchen; his wife married 2) the same day Berthold Wilbrecht,colonel(born Berlin 8.1.1902, + Muenchen in July 1976) Walter's son Hans-Otto,born Muenchen 1.8.1948,is masseur; he married Muenchen 5.4.1971 Rosemarie Kleinert,born Goldenstedt 30.10.1949; Hans-Otto has a son ...   , born Oct.1976.
c) Ernst(now Ernesto): born Villingen 16.1.1913.Became "Volkswirt".He went to Argentina(together with his brother Walter) in April 1951. He is Administrador at the Estancia La Marianita.He married Mandel(Norway) 25.6.1945 Edith Rutzen born Koeslin(Pommern) 4.2.1923.She was a daugher of Paul Rutzen(born Konikow near Koeslin 25.4.1887,+ Jarmshagen near Greifswald 17.11.1956) and of Martha Treichel,born Koeslin 25.1.1888,+ Buenos Aires 1.12.1964.

Ernst has 3 children:
1) Angelika, born Herrsching(Ammersee) 3.4.1946.She married Muenchen 18.11.1968 Manfred Steube,born Leipzig
24.7.1942,Dipl.ing. at Buenos Aires,son of the physician Fritz Steube(born Leipzig 14.7.1911) and of
Erika Simdorn(born Berlin 8.9.1919).Angelika has
3 children: Cornelia Mariana (born Reutlingen 29.5.
1970), Veronica (born Buenos Aires 28.11.1972) and
Claudia Marina (born Buenos Aires 12.5.1975)
2) Brigitte,born Herrsching 23.6.1947.She studied hygie-
nic gymnastics,married Buenos Aires 3.1.1973 Roberto
Rodolfo Campos,born Buenos Aires 30.12.1946,certi-
fied chemical engineer, son of Ricardo Ramón Campos,
expert in papers, and of Annelies Wasser.Brigitte has
a son Rodolfo Guillermo,born Buenos Aires 5.6.1975.

2) Minna: born Jestetten near Waldhut Sunday,21.1.1877, 16.00
o'clock, + Mannheim 13.9.1934 (dilatation of the heart).She
intended to become a painter,but married,at Mannheim,2.4.1903
Emanuel Gscheidlen,born Mannheim 14.10.1876, + Wiesloch 10.5.
1941,professor of Mathematics, since 1920 Oberrealschuldirek-
tor at Mannheim(with 1400 pupils the biggest scholl in Germany at this time). He was a son of Heinrich Gscheidlen,"Hauptlehrer" at Mannheim(born Babstadt 22.7.1831, + Mannheim 11.10.
1897) and of Friederike Purmann (born Schwetzingen 23.1.1839,
+ Mannheim 2.3.1920). Minna had 5 children:
a) Gertrud: born Mannheim 24.7.1904, + Wettstetten near Ingolstadt 9.3.1977. She married 1) Mannheim 6.6.1936 Willy
Henninger, reverend,then merchant,+ 22.7.1957.Divorced i n
September 1936.She married 2) Stuttgart 24.7.1941 Alfred
Meyer,Dipl.Ing. with Robert Bosch at Stuttgart(Alfred Meyer
constructed the "Bosch-Zuender"-=ignition device- and
Diesel motors for cars).He was born Augsburg 12.11.1881,
died Lindenberg(Allgaeu),where he das a house,19.6.1960.
He was a son of Carl Meyer and Emilie Aign.Gertrud had a
daughter: Monika.(Alfred Meyer had married 1)Martha Baer, x)
1)Monika was born Stuttgart 24.7.1943,married Stuttgart 1882=1934.
20.7.1963 Dieter Neumeier,Dipl.Ing,born Lindenberg(Allgaeu)16.8.1936, + Ingolstadt 2.11.1970(car accident),son
of Wilhelm Neumeier(born Hirschtal near Zweibruecken
29.7.1895,+ Kaufbeuren 30.4.1963) and of Emmy Ahlmann,
(born Wattenscheid near Bochum 28.9.1897).Monika has a
daughter Ulla,born Stuttgart 21.6.1965.
b) Wolfgang,born Mannheim 10.6.1906, became "Gartenbautech-
niker" at Stuttgart,secretary with a garden-Architect.He
married Stuttgart 3.5.1952 Hiltrud Geeck,catholic,born
Kroschnitz,Oberschlesien(=Upper Silesia),daughter of Rein-
hold Geeck,"Hauptlehrer"(born Stargard,Pommern 31.7.1868,
+ Habelschwerdt near Glatz 3.2.1941) and of Magdalena
Sczcesniak(born Gleiwitz 8.7.1882,+ Heilbronn 5.4.1957).
Children:
1)Arnulf:born Stuttgart 18.12.1953,+ Stuttgart 19.12.1953.
2) Irmhild: born Stuttgart 13.5.1955.Catholic.
Wolfgang adopted 12.4.1965 Martina,born Stuttgart 26.3.1961
(catholic,daughter of Irmgard Wilderotter,born Erbach near
Ulm 9.7.1937, and of the Greek Christoph Donon).

x) 2 children out of this marriage: Wolfgang(born 1910,professor
of Engineering research at the State College,Pennsylvania;
Karola,born 6.4.1914,doctor for children at Hamburg,married to
Leopold Boehm,Dipl.ing.

c) Mathilde,born Mannheim 12.4.1908,became "Jugenleiterin",
had a Turkish kindergarten at Izmir(Smyrna),Turkey.She
married 1) Izmir 19.6.1937 Latif Debbas(since 1934 "Debas",
the Turkish form of the name),wholesale merchant at Istanbul,born 1.3.1900 at Halep (Aleppo),Syria,+ Istanbul 13.8.
1962,son of Mehmet Debbas,wholesale merchant at Halep,
and of Ayse born Debbas.Thilde was the 4.wife of Latif.
(Latif had a daughter,Suat out of his 1.marriage with
Nadiye,Halep.This marriage was divorced. Out of his 2.Mar-
riage to Melahat + 1926 he had a son Melih).Nadiye and
Melahat were 12 years old, when they married).The father
of Latif, Mehmet, was born 22.4.1870,his wife 25.7.1876.
Mathilde(Thilde) married 2) Stuttgart 15.5.1964 Alfred
(Fred) Huttelmayer,Prokurist with the Funkberaterring
Gaensslen & Klink at Stuttgart.He was born Schwaebisch
Gmuend 15.9.1898,son of the manufacturer Karl Huttelmayer
(born Schw. Gmuend 12.6.1860,+ Schw. Gmuend 8.5.1919)
and of Lidwina Naschold (born Schw. Gmuend 23.10.1873,
+ Schorndorf 22.1.1953);he is catholic as his parents.
Fred was married 1) to Margrete Herzer(born Schw.Gmuend
17.12.1900,+ Stuttgart 16.2.1960),daughter of the manu-
facutrer Karl Herzer and of Bertha Buhl.Fred had married
1) Schw. Gmuend 25.8.1924; out of this marriage is the
daughter Ursel,born Stuttgart 9.12.1927,married Stuttgart
31.5.1949 to the tax-adviser(Steuerberater)Eduard Zapf.
(The mother of Fred Huttelmayer's great-grandfather Adam
Valentin Endres, Friederike, was a daughter of Leopoldo
Retti from Laino at the Lago di Como,Italy; Leopoldo Retti built the castle at Stuttgart in the years 1746-1751;
the brother of Retti's mother,Donato Giuseppe Frisoni,
built the town of Ludwigsburg and its castle 1712-1734).
Thilde had a son,Ferid, born Istanbul 27.2.1943, + Ismae-
lia,Egypt 26.1.1947 (infection of the intestins and per-
nicious anema); he was buried at the Mohammedan cemetery
of Port Said.
d) Hedwig (Hedi),born Mannheim 12.4.1910,became "Kindergaert-
nerin", had an own kindergarten at Ludwigshafen.She married Mannheim 12.8.1937 Hans Walch,Oberstudienrat at
Eberbach(Neckar),since 1960 - 1973 at the Studienkolleg
at Heidelberg,preparing pupils from other countries for
the Abitur in Germann.He was born Mannheim 27.7.1908,as
son of Johann Christoph Walch,Hauptlehrer at Mannheim(born
Gemmingen 19.11.1879,+ Mannheim 29.1.1955) and of Emilie
Cassin (born Mannheim 26.3.1882,+ Mannheim 1.2.1957.Her
great-grandfather,Jean-Baptiste Cassin was attorney at
the court of justice at Sedan,France;he was married to
Margarete Rognon).-Common ancestor of Hedi (9 generations
back) and Hans (8 generations back) was Daniel Wilhelmi
(born Marburg 28.8.1631). Hedi has 4 children:
1) Johannes(Hannes),born Mannheim 21.5.1938.Forester at
Schoemberg near Freudenstadt.He married Luebeck 17.8.
1963 Christa Foerster,born Luebeck 12.1.1942,daughter
of Karl Foerster,Installateur(=plomber),born 28.4.1897,
and of Maria Duennebeil,born 8.10.1903. Hannes has 3
children: Matthias(born Eberbach/Neckar 2.7.1964,
Freudenstadt
Christian (born 16.6.1966) and Ulrike (born Freudenstadt 25.2.1968).

2) Klaus,born Mannheim 22.5.1940,Praeparator since 1960
at the Senckenberg-Museum in Frankfurt(Main).He married Mammolshain near Koenigstein(Taunus) 31.5.1968
Iris Kramer,born Frankfurt(Main) 24.12.1942,daughter
of Friedrich Kramer(born 16.7.1914) and of Margot
Knauf(born 1.2.1917,divorced,married 2) to Hans Pfaff,
mayor of Mammolshain).1975 Klaus became leader of the
branch "palaeontology" of the museum.
3) Heidi-Doris,born Stuttgart 19.4.1942,became Kindergaert-
nerin,then she played together with the famous puppet-
players of Hohnstein as well as her future husband,
Guenter Lipski,whom she married at Eberbach(Neckar)
9.6.1965.He was born Marienburg 8.9.1935,son of Otto
Lipski,master of orthopaedy(born 21.9.1904 Garnsee
near Marienwerder) and of Emma Jaeger(born Wossarken
near Graudenz 13.2.1909).Guenter Lipski became Hauptlehrer at Eberbach(Neckar). Heidi-Doris has a son
Nicolai,born Eberbach(Neckar) 30.3.1967.
4) Angelika (Angi),born Mannheim 5.3.1954,became nurse
for babies.She married Waldkatzenbach near Eberbach/N.
13.8.1977 Ralf Zelch,stud.phys.,born Gladbeck 24.9.
1953,son of Martin Zelch (born Reußdorf,Siebenbuergen
16.9.1922) and of Eva Blaschke(born Breslau 18.12.1926)
e) Ilse,born Mannheim 4.4.1914,became chief-secretary at
Chocolat Tobler at Stuttgart,in the department for pub-
licity(Werbe-Abteilung).

3) Hermann: born Mannheim 13.3.1889, + Muenchen 6.3.1950,became
pianist.He was Dr. of philosophy,pedagogy and musical science
since 1916.He was too musical critic at the newspaper "Muanch-
ner Post".He married Muenchen 26.8.1919 Hedwig Mauerer,born
Muenchen 10.12.1888,singer at the opera under the name "Hedwig Gluth"She was a daughter of Georg Mauerer(born Muenchen
26.11.1858, + Muenchen 12.1.1947,chief administrator of the
local sickfund at Muenchen) and of Emilie Gluth (born Bay-
reuth 8.9.1863, + Muenchen 17.12.1924).

Supplement

Children of Wilhelm Wilhelmi born 1819:

a) Heinrich: geb̶n̶ born 23.11.1851 Heddesbach, + Hamburg 16.2.1919,
married Colmar/Alsace 14.6.1884 to Eugénie Johner,
born Muenster/Alsace 15.5.1856, + Beblenheim/Alsace
24.10.1911. 8 children:
   1) Elisabeth,born Parchim 18.4.1886,+ Hamburg 7.8.1943,
   married Hamburg 5.3.1913 to Gustav Kammerer,born Hamburg 21.6.1857,+ Hamburg 25.9.1942,public prosecutor
   2) Heinrich,born Guestrow 25.4.1888,pastor at Hamburg,
   + St.Peter 21.5.1968,married Rellingen 20.11.1922 to
   Sophie Bitterling,born Kollmar/Elbe 24.10.1894.
   The son Friedrich-Wilhelm(born 18.7.1931 St.Peter)
   became "Amtsgerichtsrat" at Hamburg; the son Christoph
   (born Hamburg 4.12.1934) became publishers-merchant
   3) Friedrich-Wilhelm,born Guestrow 3.9.1889,killed in
   the 1.world-war 20.2.1915,lieutenant
   4) Peter,born Guestrow 25.10.1890,+ La Guaira(Venezuela)
   18.4.1950,merchant
   5) Friedrich-Franz,born Guestrow 19.3.1892,+ 10.8.1960
   near Montabaur by a car- accident,pastor at Muehlhau-
   sen(Thuringia),married Hamburg 27.8.1926 to Elisabeth
   Schaefer(born Hamburg 1.1.1907).-The son Kaspar(born
   Hamburg 24.7.1927,+ Hamburg 1.10.1963) was architect;
   the son Peter (born Gross-Treben 3.8.1928) became
   "Oberregierungsrat"; the son Gerhard(born Muehlhausen,
   Thuringia 6.3.1938) became Pastor at Obernjesa; the son
   Friedrich(born Muehlhausen 23.5.1942) is mecanician
   for motor vehicles.
   6) Cornélie,born Guestrow 26.9.1893,+ Hamburg 10.6.1949,
   married Hamburg 15.5.1918 to Carl Bertheau,born Hamburg 4.7.1878, + Hamburg 12.11.1944,"Studienrat".
   7) Anna,born Guestrow 28.12.1894,married Hamburg 22.12.1924
   1924 to Wilhelm Muhs,born Kiel 10.4.1895,+ Elmshorn 10.7.
   1976,"Studienrat"
   8) Philipp,born Hamburg 16.6.1898,+ Merida (Venezuela)
   15.3.1925,merchant.
b) Ludwig: born Heddesbach 14.1.1855, + Rostock 15.4.1923, pastor at
Brunow,married Berlin 28.10.1886 to Lonny Neumann,born
Danzig 14.1.1849, + Marlow 13.1.1923
c) Axel: born Heddesbach 13.11.1857, + Schwerin 20.6.1928.Dr.med. at
Dassow,then Guestrow,at last Obermedizinalrat at Schwerin.
Married Dassow 10.10.1882 to Helene Rahe,born Luebtheen
14.3.1855, + Schwerin 11.11.1930
His son Axel(born Dassow 24.10.1884,+ Rio de Janeiro about
1952) was merchant.
His son Curt(born Schwerin 11.1.1894) was Dr. med.,was killed in the 2. world-war in 1942 at Greece
d) Paul: born Luebz 15.10.1860,+ 18.3.1940,became "Fortsrechnungsrat"
at Schwerin.He married 7.11.1889 Martha Jaeger,born Eisen-
ach 18.6.1862,+ Buetzow 12.11.1935
e) Helene: born Ludwigslust 8.3.1863,+ Rostock 28.3.1940,married Kote-
low 24.4.1896 to Friedrich Voss,reverend,born Krakow 3.8.
1859,+ Rostock 10.3.1954
f) Marie: born Brudersdorf 4.8.1867,+ Paris 9.7.1893,married Guestrow
27.9.1889 to Friedrich Voss(later husband of Helene)
g) Karl: born Brudersdorf 16.10.1871,+ Illzach,Alsace 21.11.1944.
"Oberleutnant" and merchant.Married 1) Muenchen 10.10.1899 to
Marion Einstein,born Muenchen 6.5.1874,+ 6.11.1929,divorced
1918.2) toMargarete Anna Mueller,born Breitenbach 14.8.1890,
+ Muehlhausen,Alsace 19.6.(1938?)

Julius Wilhelmi was born Stebbach 16.7.1823, + Washington/Mo 24.1.1883.
He married 1) (Oct.?) 1852 Luise Landfried,+ 1861,
before the 7.10. He married 2) (1872?) Henriette
Heistermann of Schoetmar(Lippe). Children:
1) Otto: born Grays Summit,Mo 20.8.1853,architect at
   St.Louis.Married to Emilie Stiefel,daughter of
   Christoph Stiefel and Emilie ... Otto had 6 children:
   a) Julius:born 18.4.1884, + January 1897.
   b) Gertrud: born 22.8.1886, + 21.5.1969, married
      to Dr. Theodore Hempelmann,pediatrician at St.
      Louis,+ 13.12.1943. The daughter Marion Paula
      (born 1916) married 14.6.1940 Roger Hampton
      (her children:Randall,born 1943,married Karla,is
       living at Houston/Texas; Betty Jean,born 1947,mar
       ried George Baker,Texas).
   c) Paula: born 4.4.1888,teacher,married Frank Moody,
      teacher. No issue.
   d) Tillie(Ottilie): born 24.12.1889, + 26.12.1964,
      married Richard Gildehaus jr.,born 1886,+ 10.6.
      1968.Children: Richard III(born 1915,+ 23.10.
      1959,married to Mary Alice Grant; son Richard IV
      is born 1944)married Karen Sue Rockwell), and
      Emilie(born 1919,married to Walter Mayer,St.
      Louis,born 1918; daughter Sally Anne,born 1948,
      is married to William Lee Derrick born 1947,has
      a son Bradley born 1970)
   e) Otto: born 16.10.1892,Dr.,urologist.Married 1)
      to Alleen Dunn,2) to Ruth Fisse. 3 children:
      Patricia(born 1925,married to Jack Franklin;
      children Cherise born 1953 and Michele born 1956).
      Grace(born 1929,married to Robert Craig; child-
      ren Calvin born 1961 and Cynthia born 1966)
      Dennis (born 1934,married to Josephine La Fata;
      children Dennis born 1956, Susan born 1959 and
      Marie born 1961).
   f) Curt: born 7.12.1894,married to Hazel Judd
      + 1970. 2 children:
      Robert(born 1923,married to Bonnie Chappel,
      born 1926.Children:Curt born 1953, and Candi
      born 1956)
      Alyce (born 1928, married to Robert Pritchard,
      Salem/Oregon.Children Jeffrey born 1950, and
      the daughters Jody born 1953 and Jamin born
      1957)
2) Emilie: born 8.8.1855, + July 1902,married 1878
   to Friedrich W. Stumpe,banker at Washington/Mo.
   4 children:
   a) Erna: born Washington/Mo 1879, + 1941,married
      1900 to the publisher J.N. Tankersley born 1871,
      + 1938..She had the children Normand (born 1903.
      No issue), Aenid Emilie(born 1907,lawyer,married
      1923 to the lawyer Chalmer C.Taylor.XChildren
      Taylor: James,born 1928,Dr.of philosophy,married
      1951,1 daughter, 1 son; and Stephen C.,born
      1932,lawyer,married 1956, 2 daughters, 1 son)
      and Robert(born 1909. No issue)
      x)since January 1967 San Diego,12094 Callado Road

(Julius Wilhelmi)
Supplement
b) Ada(Adele):born at Washington/Mo
   married to Guy Jurden. No issue.
c) Robert: born at Washington/Mo
d) Elsie: born at Washington/Mo, Married to ...
   Ritter. No issue.

3) Ida Luise: born 23.3.1857 Washington/Mo.
4) Katharina(Ketha): born Washington/Mo 24.9.1861.
   Married to Georg Marsh,pharmacist at Sand Diego,
   California.2 children:
   a) Otto: born Washington/Mo San Diego,California.
   b) Modesta: Born San Diego,California,+ 1965,
      married to Elmer Baxter,SanDiego. Children Robert
      and Roberta.
5) Helene(out of the 2.marriage of Julius): born
   Washington/Mo 5.1.1873

Franz Wilhelmi,born Stebbach 18.2.1827, + Washington/Mo 28.1.1883.
Children:
a) Anna, born Labaddie,Mo 2.7.1851: see page 66!
b) Max: born Labaddie 5.11.1852.Florist at Lawrence,Kansas.Married
   19.1.1879 to Emma Johanna Gallenkamp,born Washington/Mo 13.10.
   1854,daughter of + Wilhelm Gallenkamp from Lippe and Maria
   Stumpe. 6 children:
   1) Henilie: born Lawrence 26.7.1881,married Sept.1909 to
      William Underhill Moore,prof.of law at the university of
      Kansas,then Madison/Wisconsin,Chicago,Columbia/New Aork City.
      Daughter Elda Alwine,born 20.8.1909
   2) Alwine:born Lawrence 23.11.1883.Was living in Long Beach,
      California in 1966
   3) Alice: born Lawrence 3.4.1886,married to Floyd Doubleday,
      4100 Locust Street,Kansas City,Mo.
   4) Max:born Lawrence 19.12.1888
   5) Irma)
   6) Ilsa)born Lawrence 20.10.1894
c) Clara:born Washington/Mo 2.2.1854,married 23.4.1872 to Hermann
   Wiesel,Denver/Colorado,born Wiesbaden 28.10.1844.3 children:
   1) Joseph: born 23.4.1875, commercial traveler,Denver,Colorado
   2) Paul:born 4.9.1876,medical doctor at Garfield,Washington
   3) Franziska:born 13.3.1887
d) Minna: born Washington/Mo 1.5.1858.Married 20.6.1878 to Joseph
   H.Schmidt,Washington/Mo,born Blumberg(Baden) 17.3.1852.Children:
   1) Elmar,born 9.7.1879, + 3.5.1963,optician at Washington/Mo.
      His wife ... soon died after him. His son has a jewelry store
      at Washington,Mo.Elmer spoke and read German fluently.
   2) Alwine Josephine: born 9.10.1882, married 4.10.1905 to Walter
      Stumpe at Washington,Mo.The Daughter Elda Alwine was born
      1.5.1907.
e) Alwine: born 18.8.1858 Washington/Mo.,married Heidelberg 24.12.
   1884 Joseph Stamer,born Boehl(Rheinpfalz) 13.9.1846,"Oberregierungsrat" at Reutlingen. 3 children:
   1) Erna:born Neresheim 9.12.1885
   2) Max: born Neresheim 9.4.1887,"Oberarzt" at Reutlingen, killed
      in the 1. world-war.
   3) Clara: born Balingen 24.9.1891(1894?)

Made in the USA
Lexington, KY
10 March 2014